Artwork and Design by Michael Errigo
Edited by **Carissa Pardee**

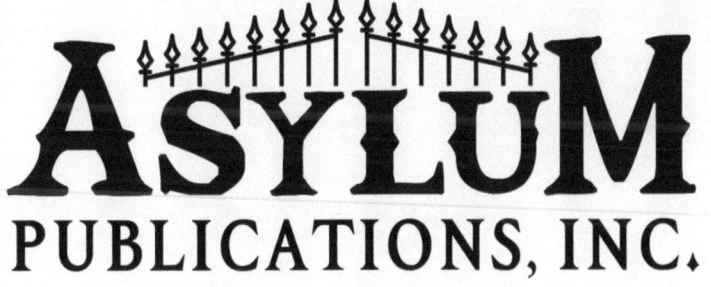

CEO and Publisher **Paul Burke**

ISBN: 978-1-7363197-7-2

Treasures of Inspiration ™. Published by Asylum Publications, Inc. ™ © Michael Errigo. Asylum Publications, Inc. logo TN 2023. All rights reserved. No portion of this publication may be reproduced or transmitted, in any form by any means, without written consent from the Publisher, except for any small excerpts for the purpose of review. For further information regarding custom photo/art books, ordering wholesale, or other inquiries, please write to asylumpublications75@gmail.com. www.asylumpublications.com
Michael Errigo   m.errigo@yahoo.com

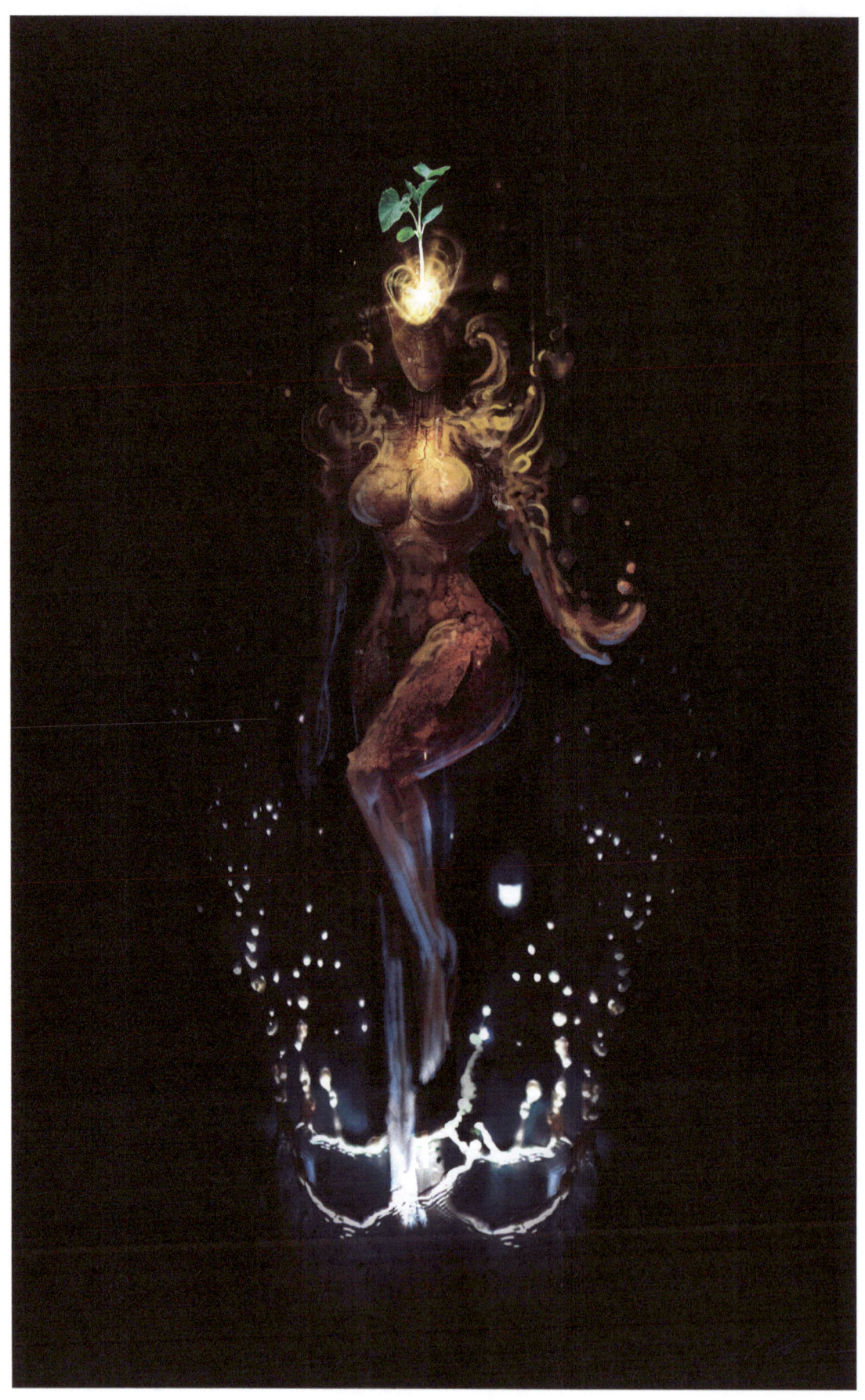

Durt

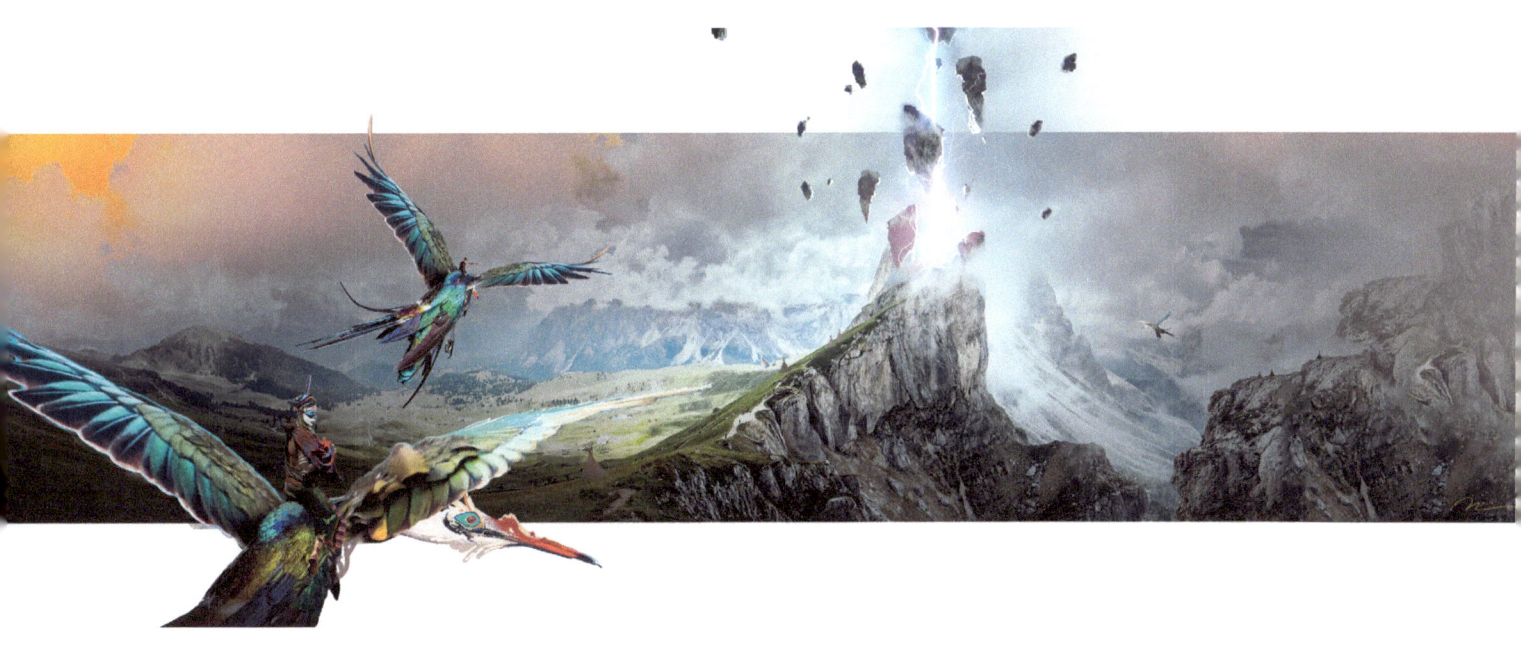

Other Worlds 1

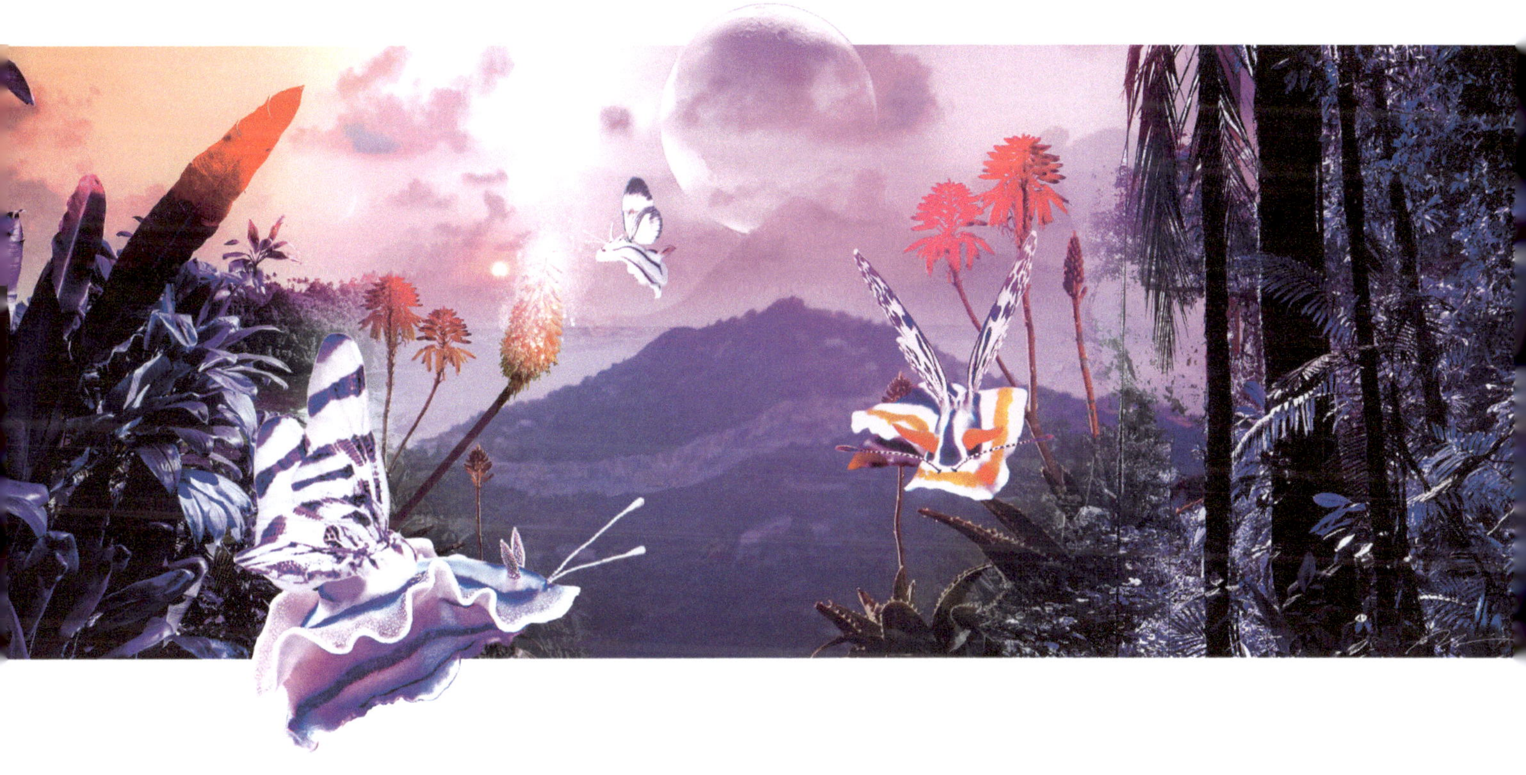

Other Worlds 2

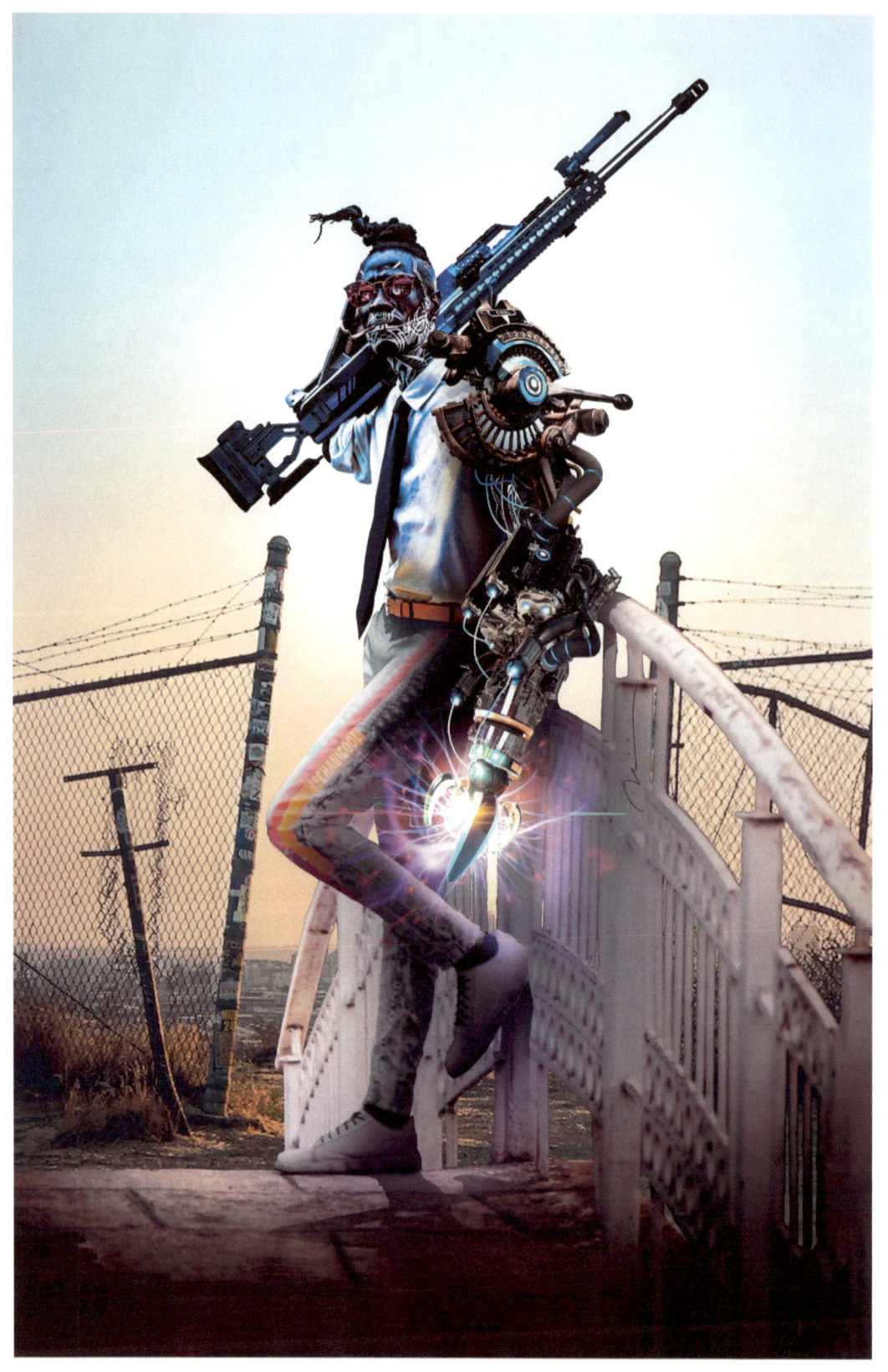

MechaniCool

Living in the gutter in the year 2222, he has been adding to his mechanical arm with scrap pieces that he can afford or that he finds. He aspires to soon be able to afford many upgrades with brand new cyberware, including a new energy blaster.

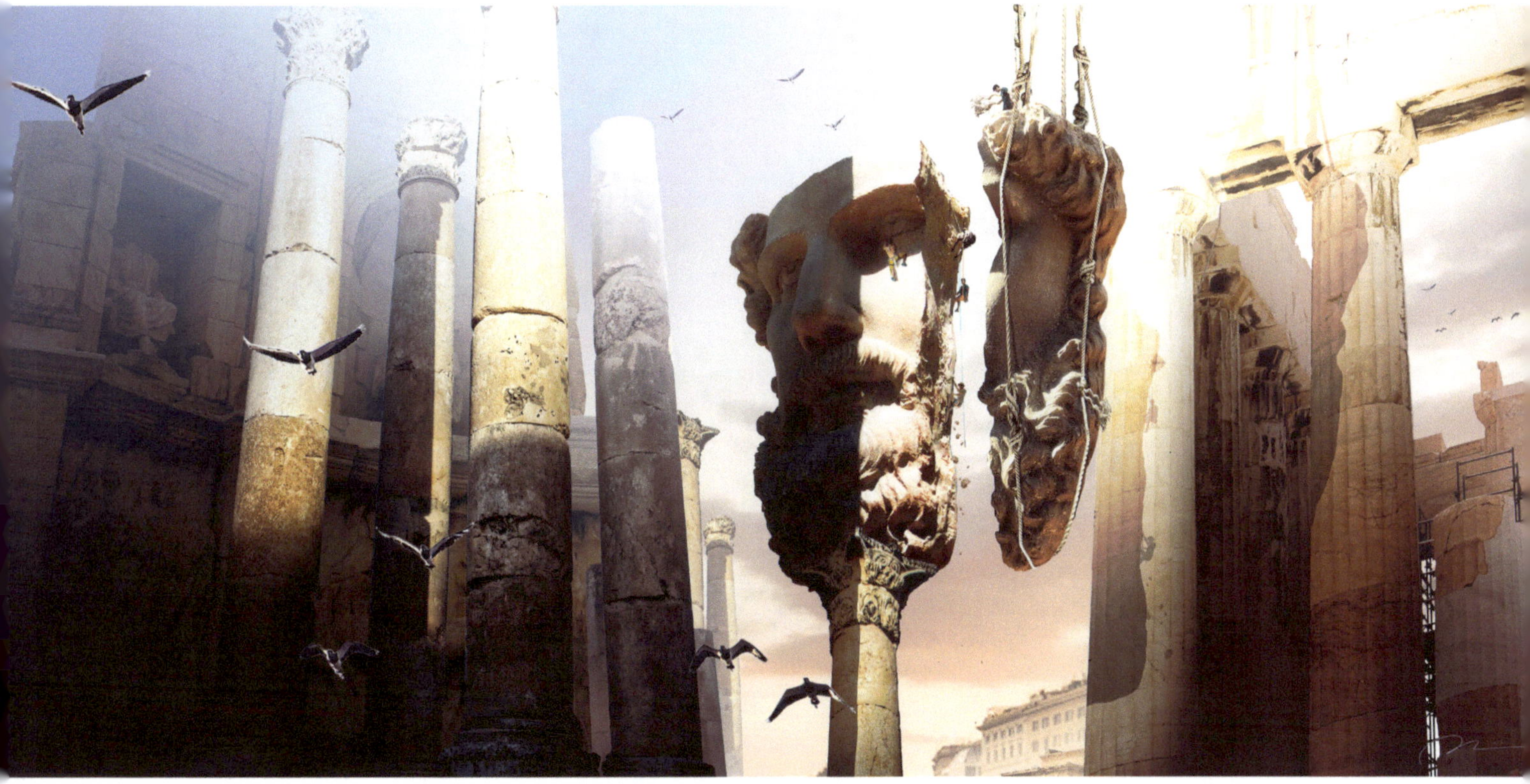

Re-building Rome

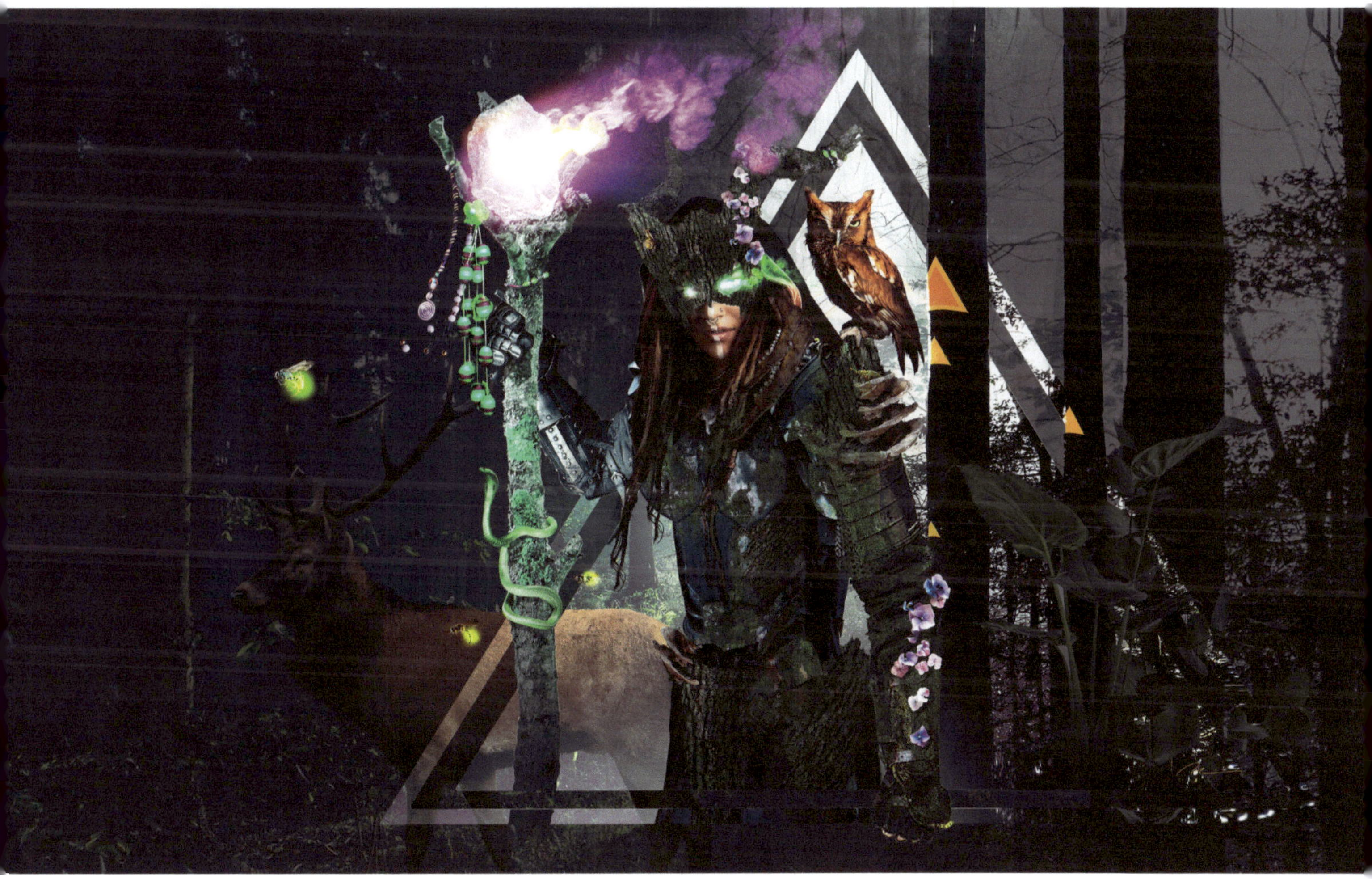

Forest Druid

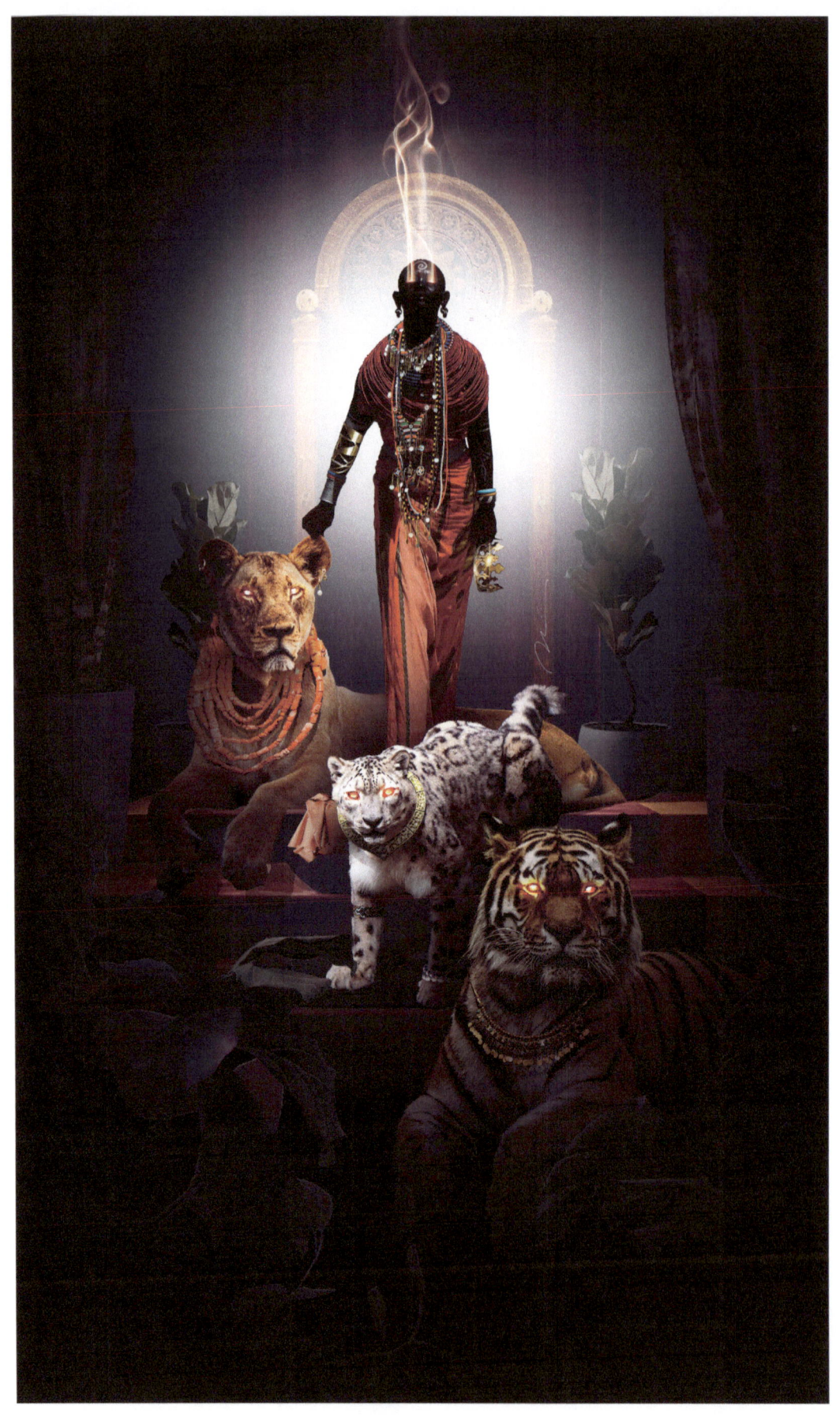

Jungle Queen

The Jungle Queen and her three best friends.

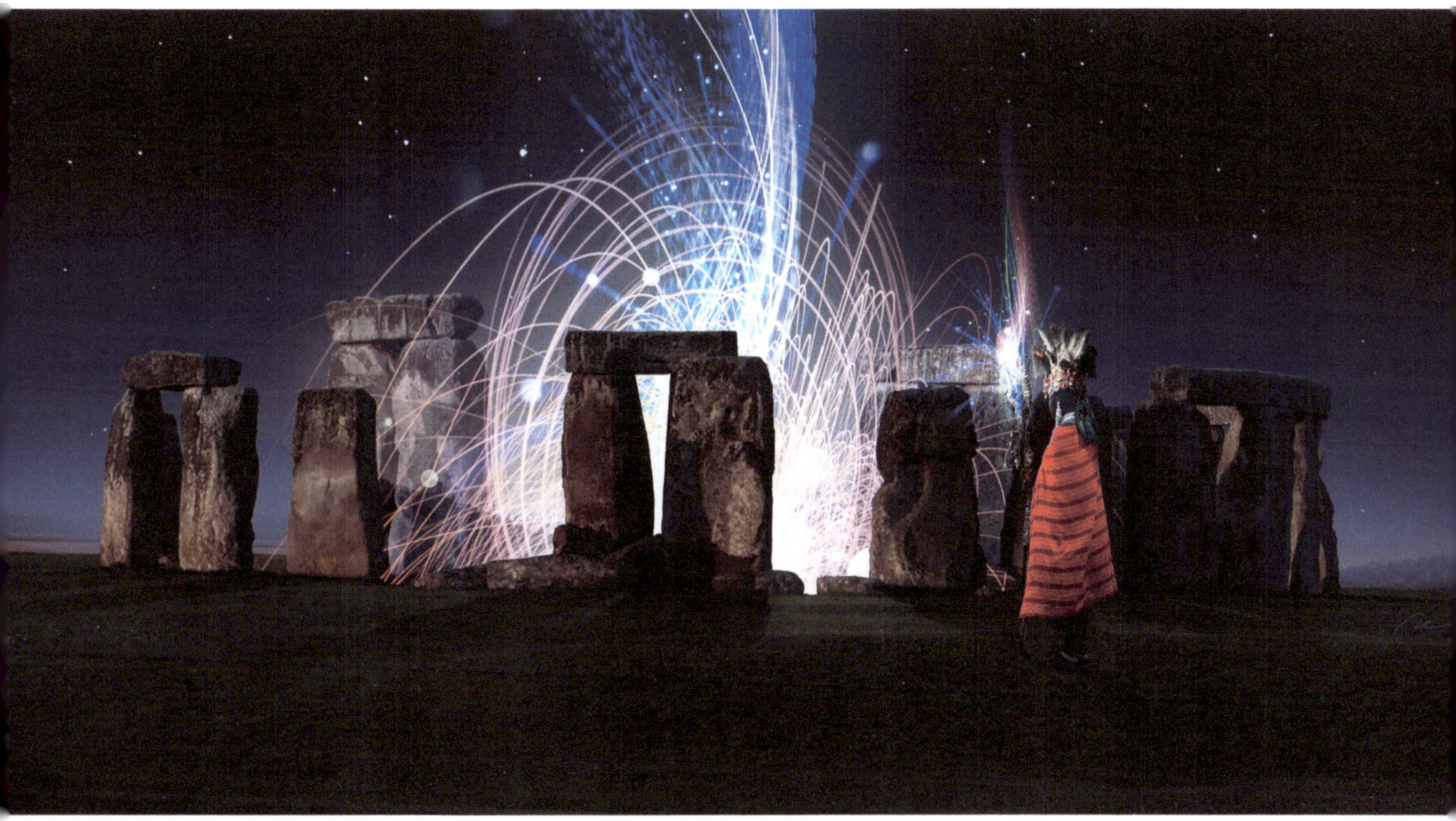

Stonehenergy

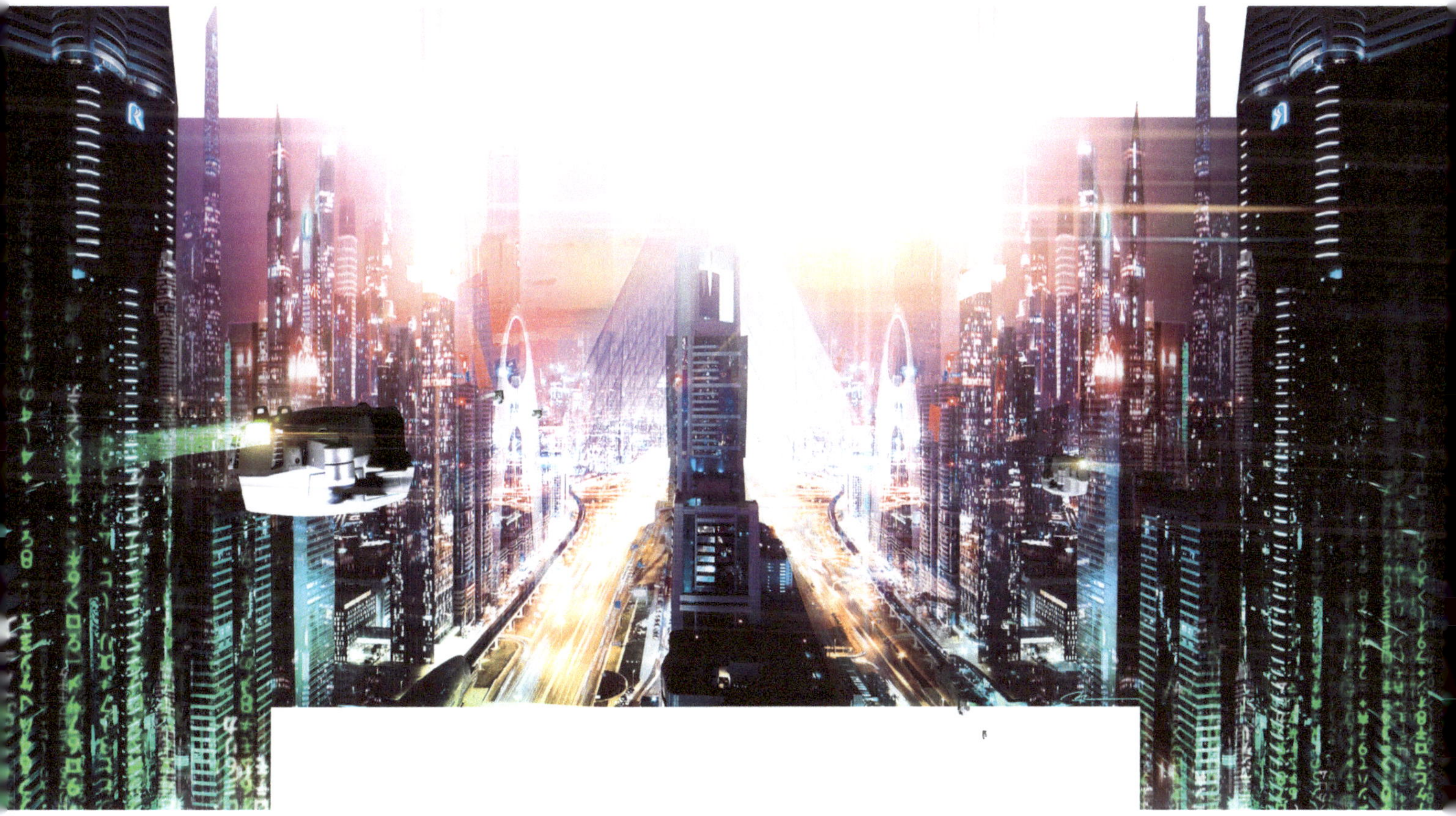

Matrix City

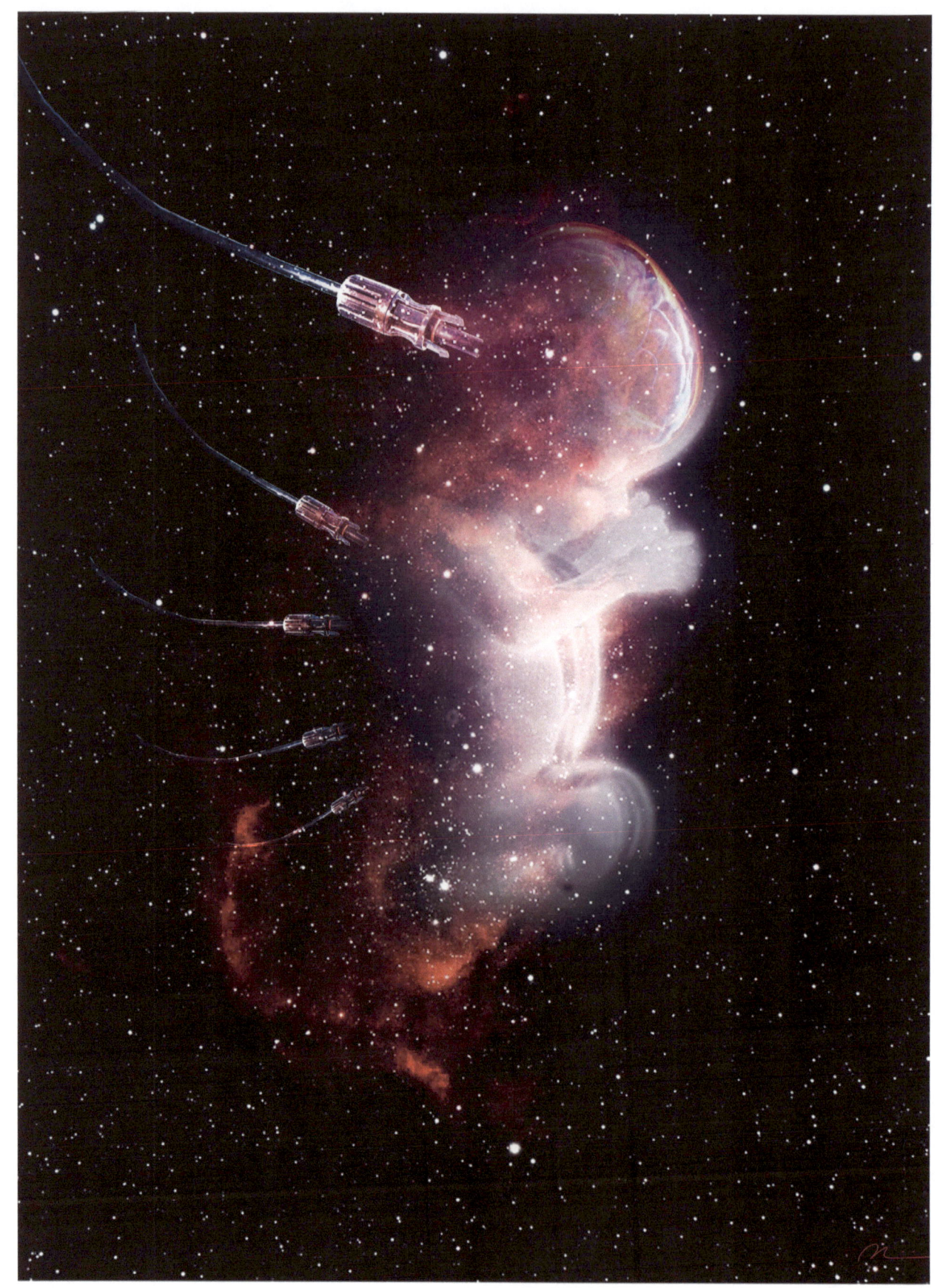

Star Boy

A child born amongst the stars but plugged into a system of control.

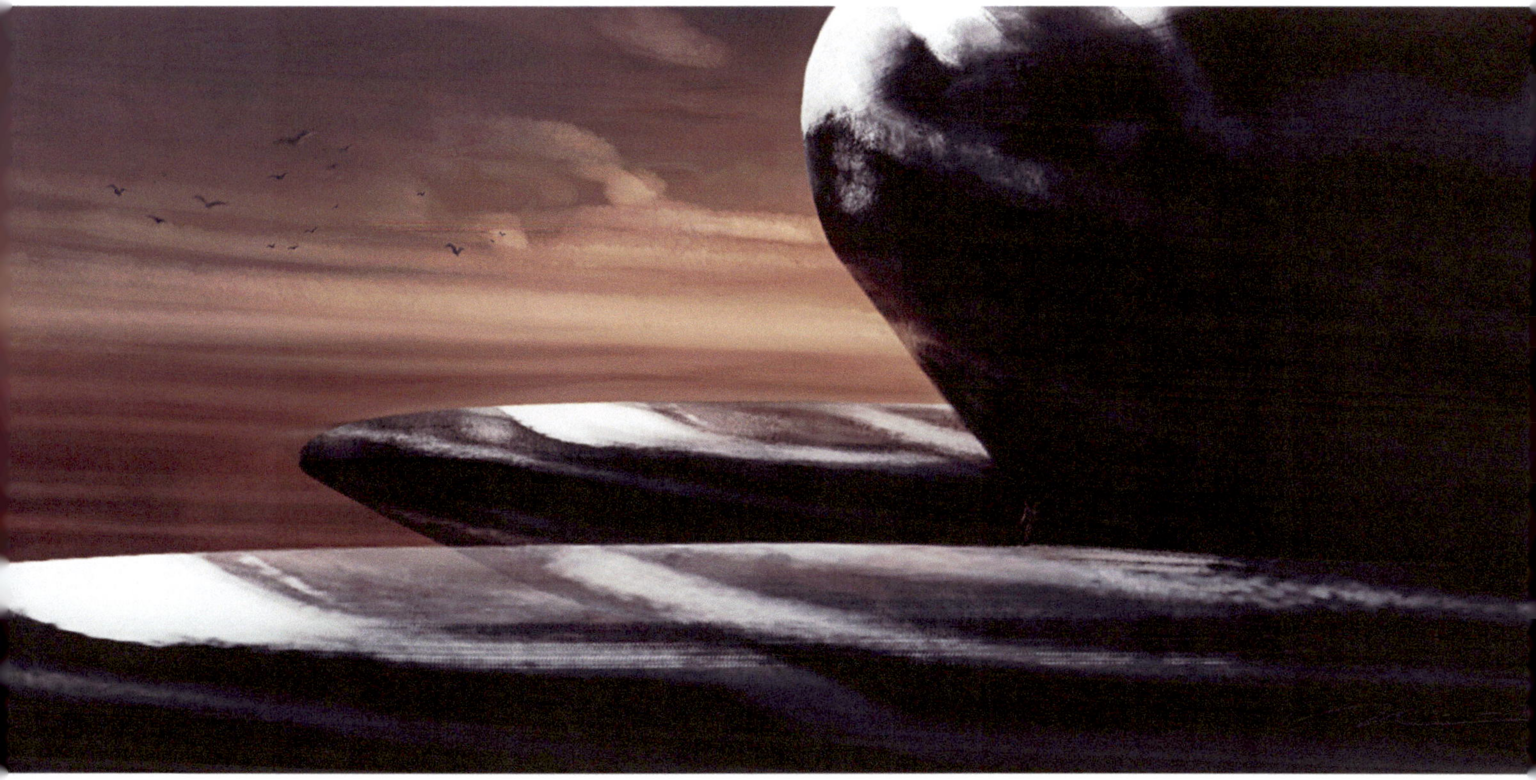

Explorer

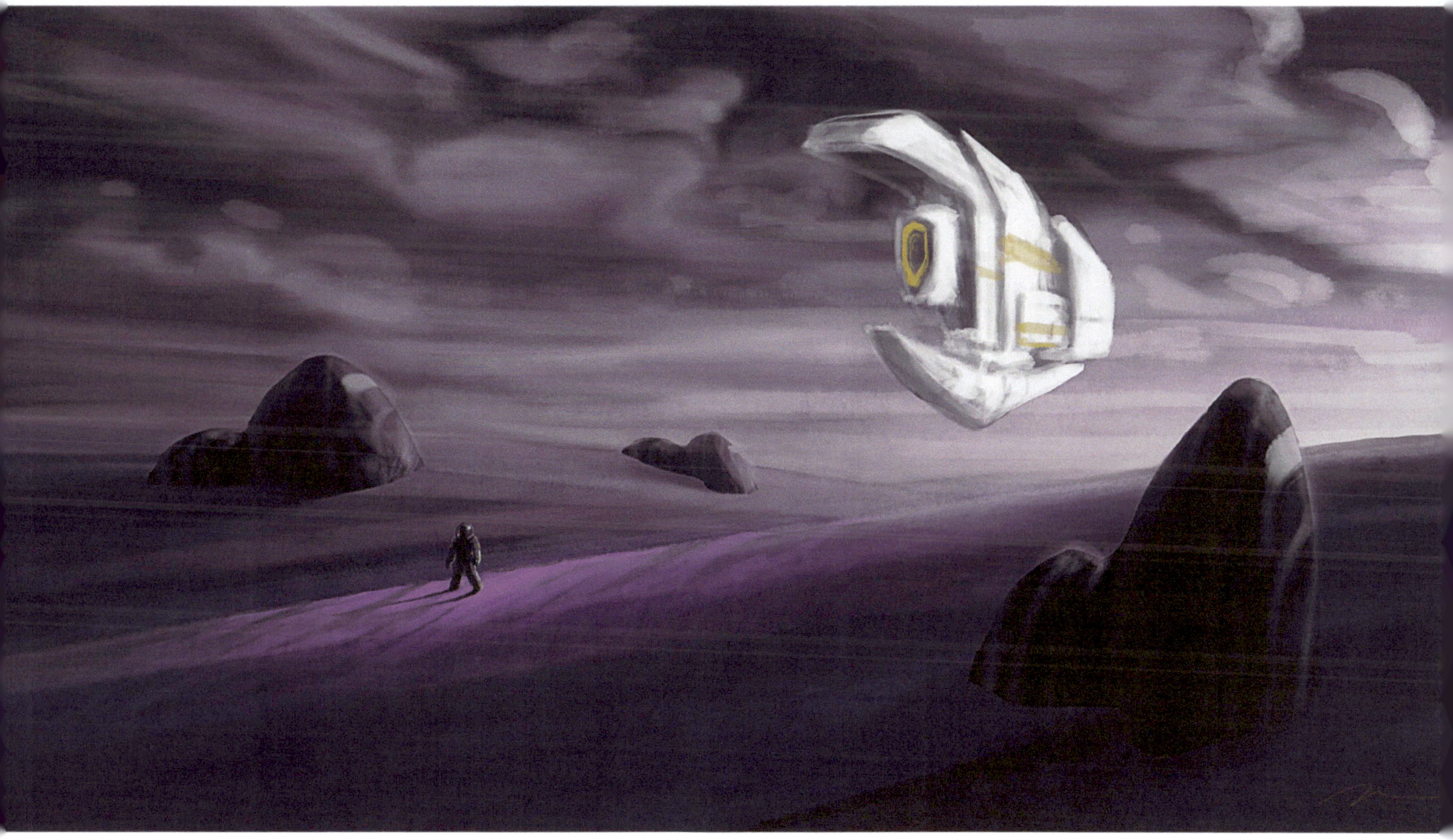

Alien Planet

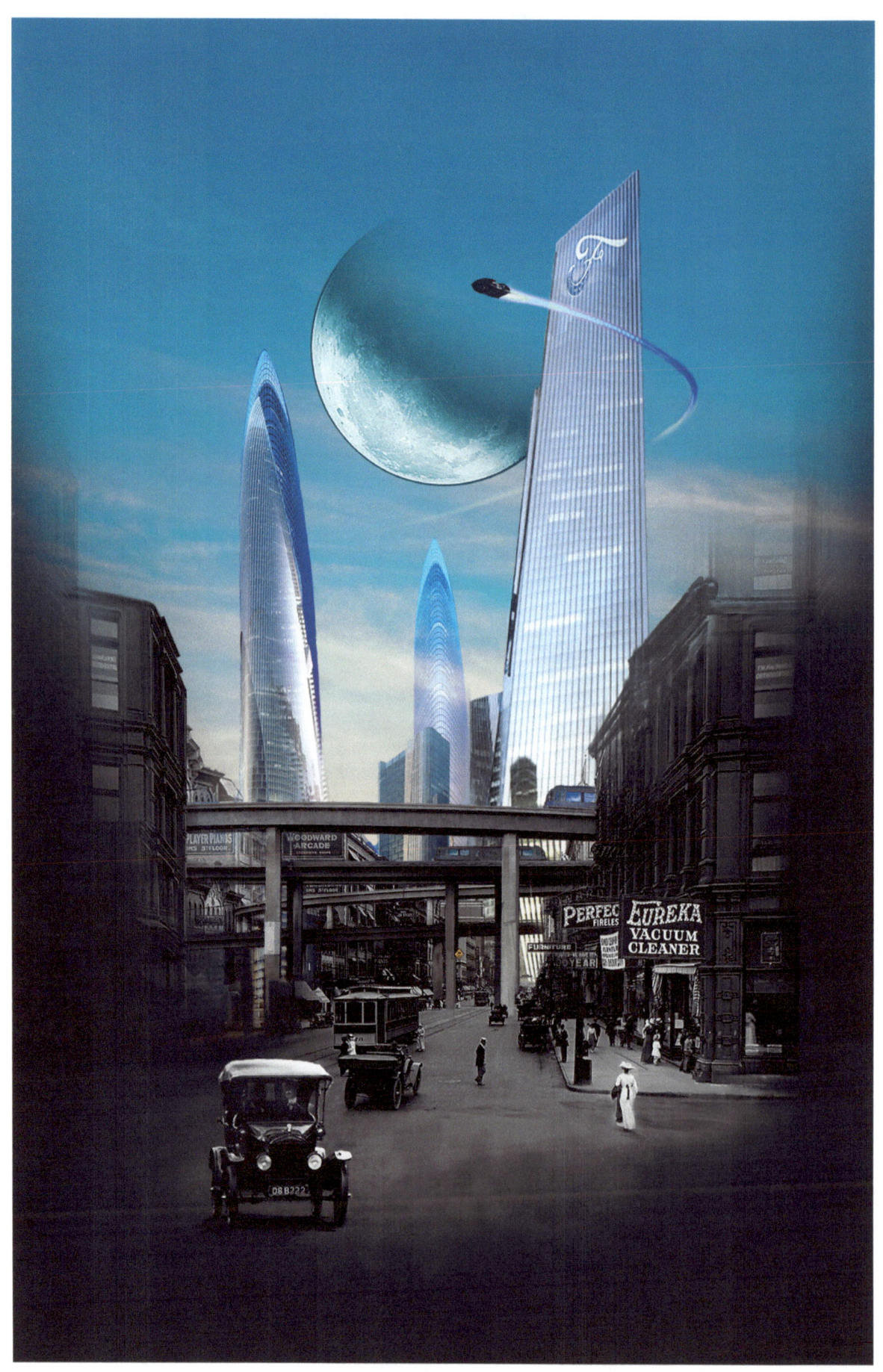

Into The Future

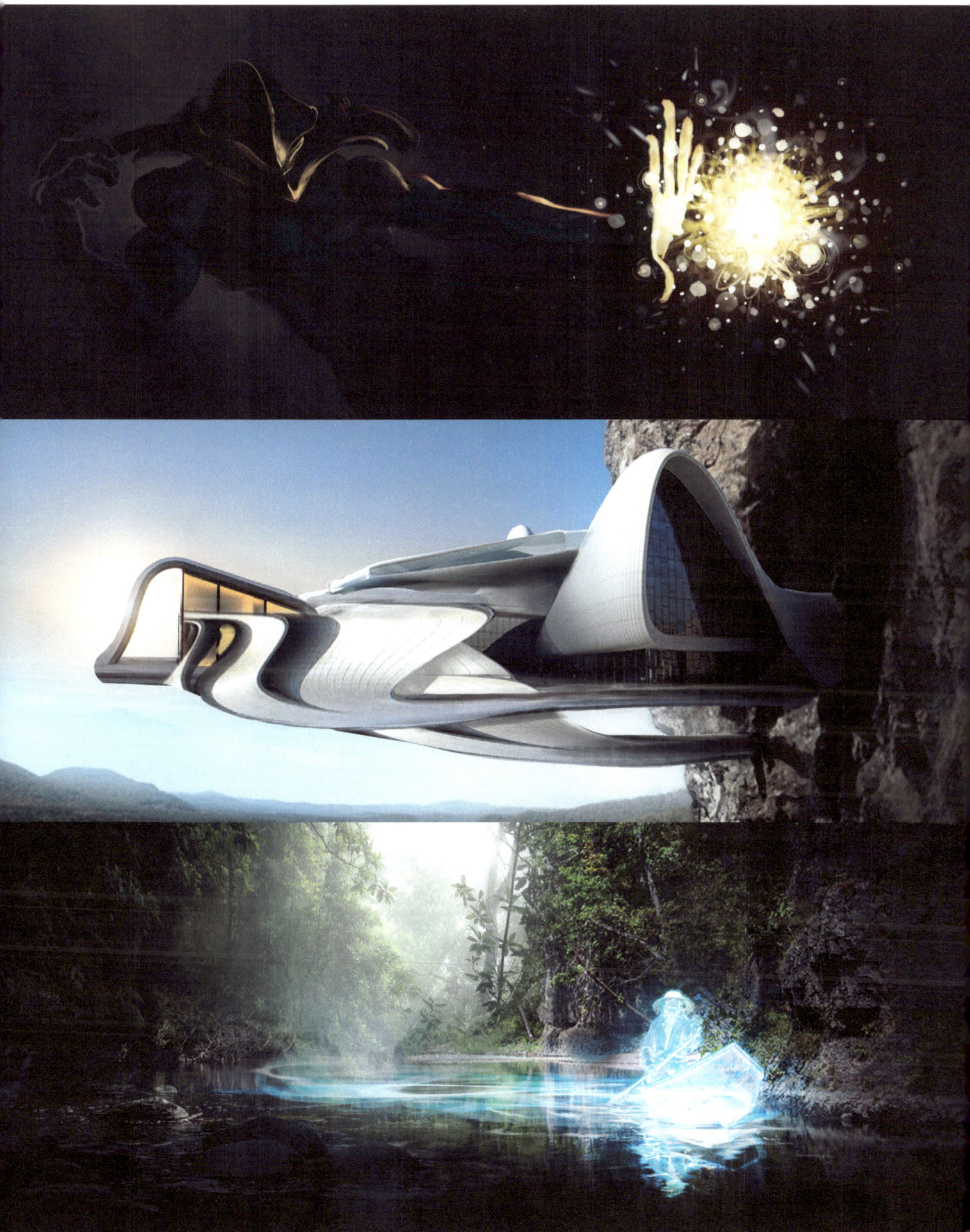

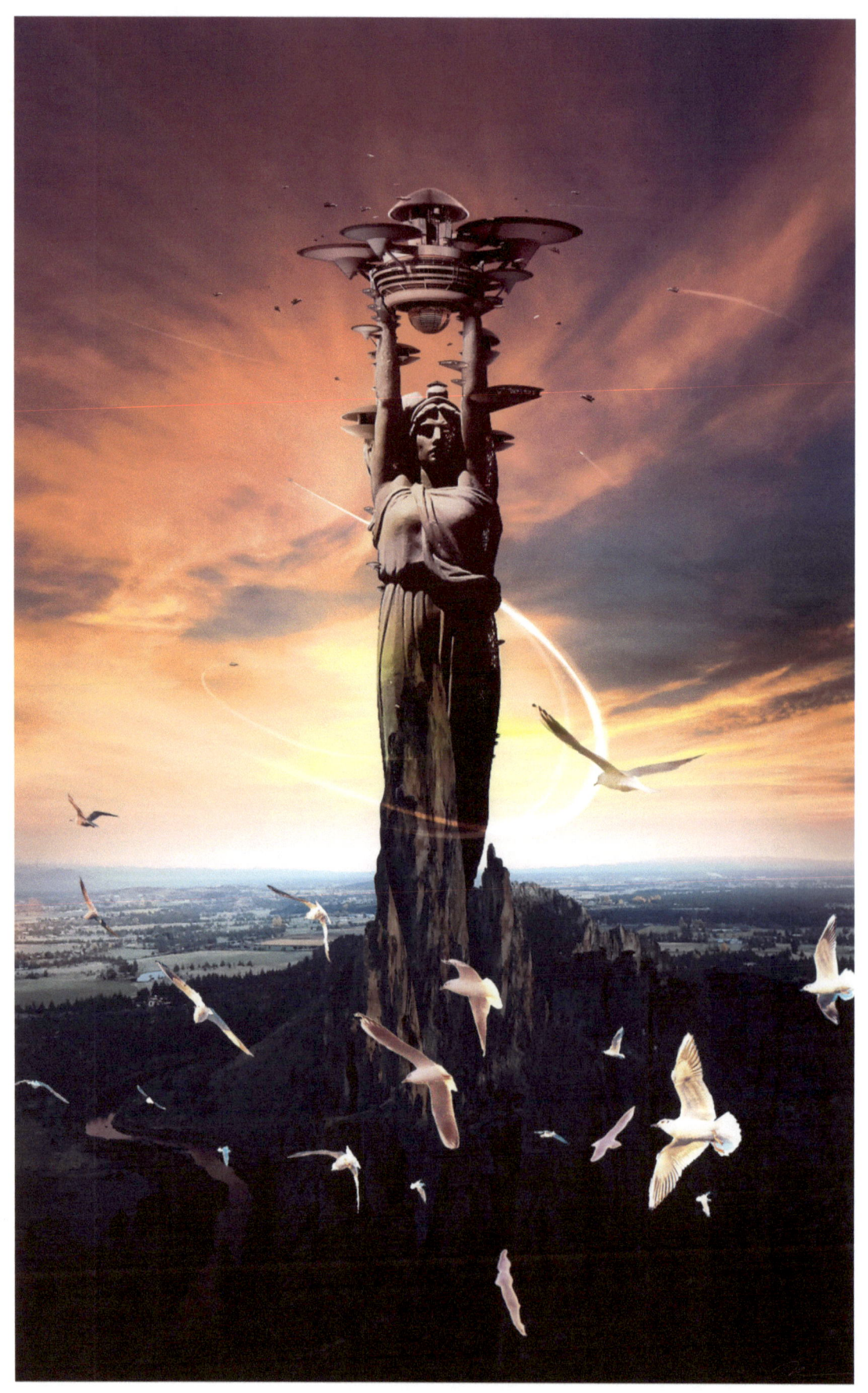

Statue City

Stribe, New Crib, Glow Boat Joe
(previous page)

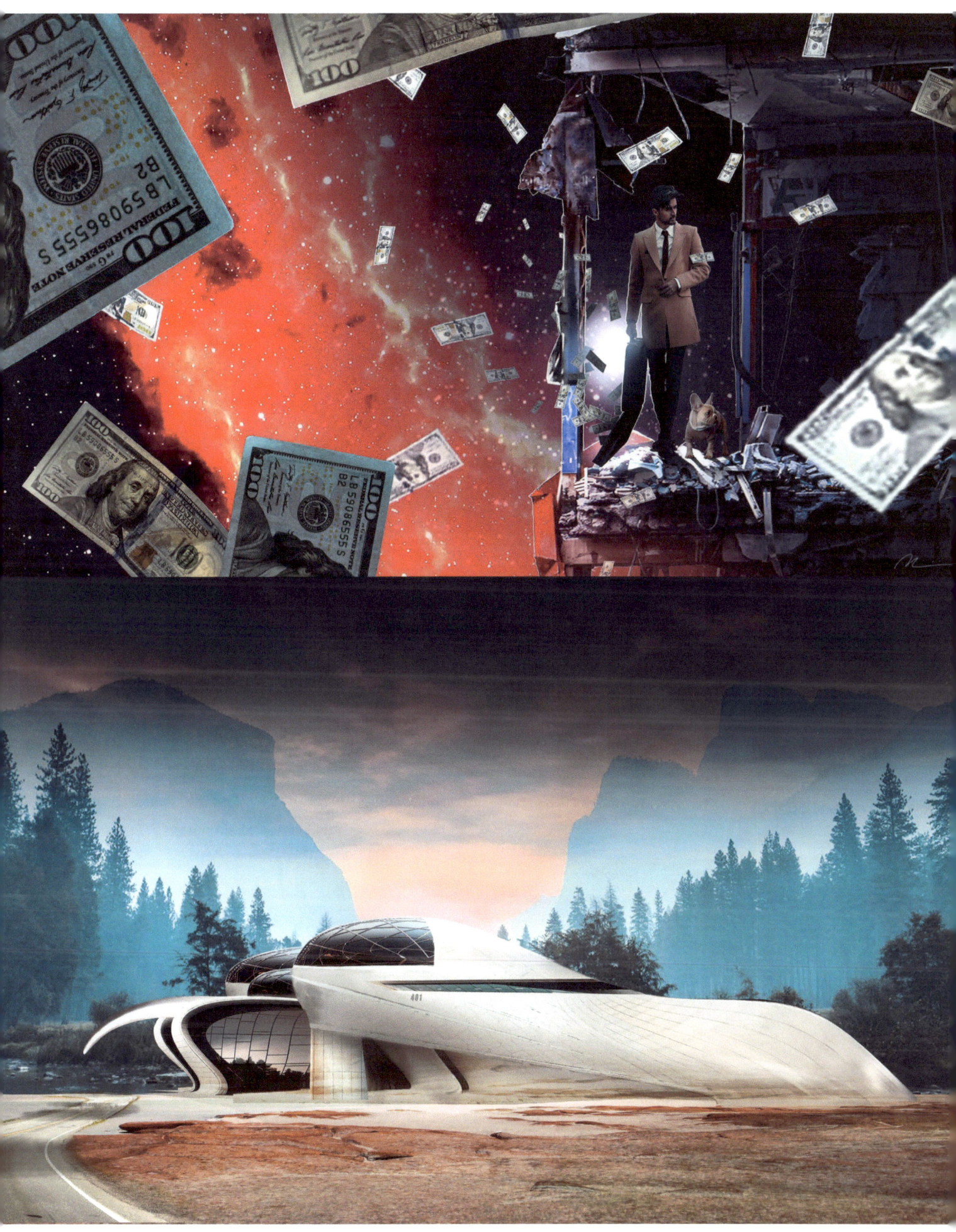

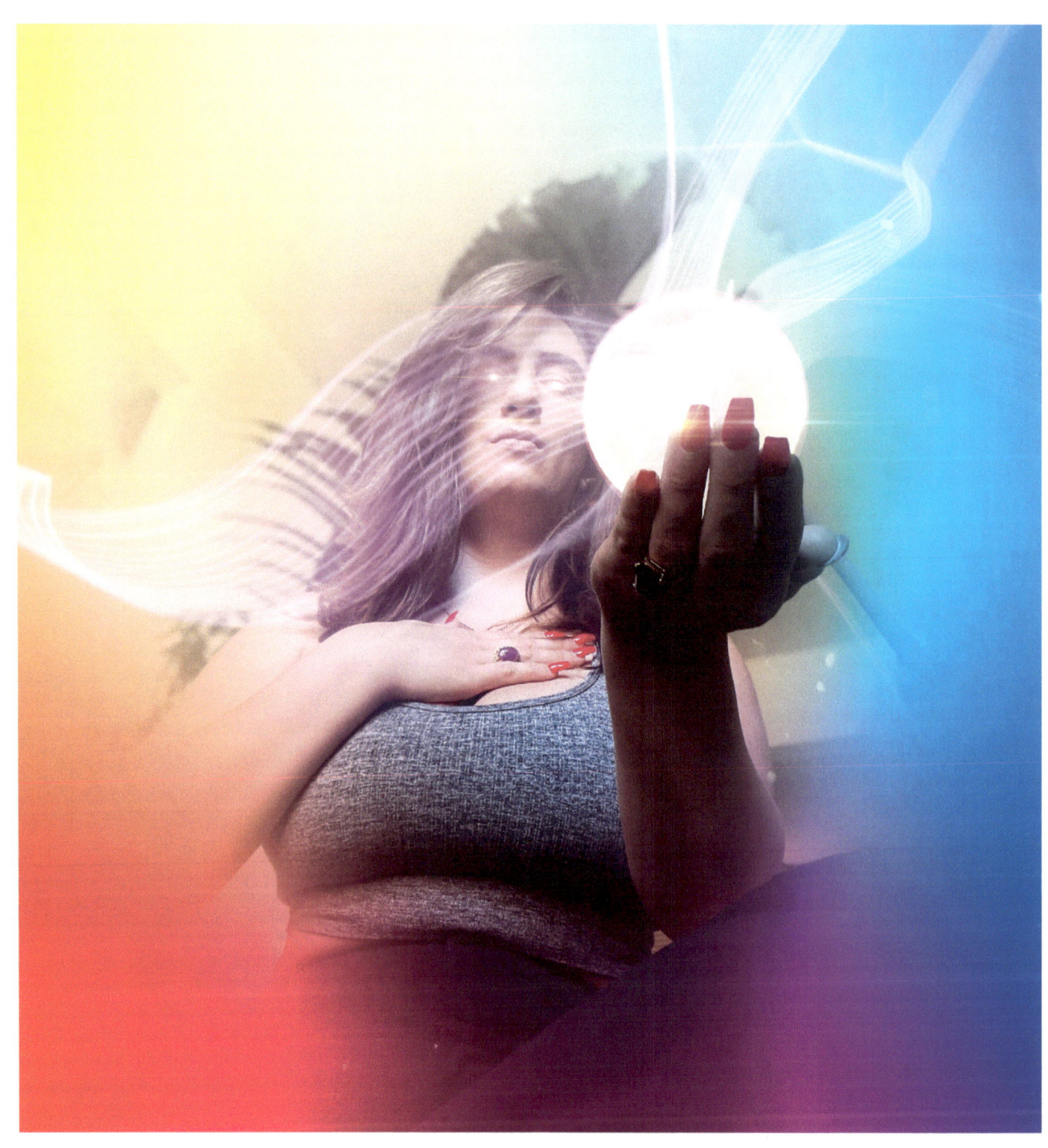

Reihi with Yvonne 1

Money Lost, Hospital 401
(previous page)

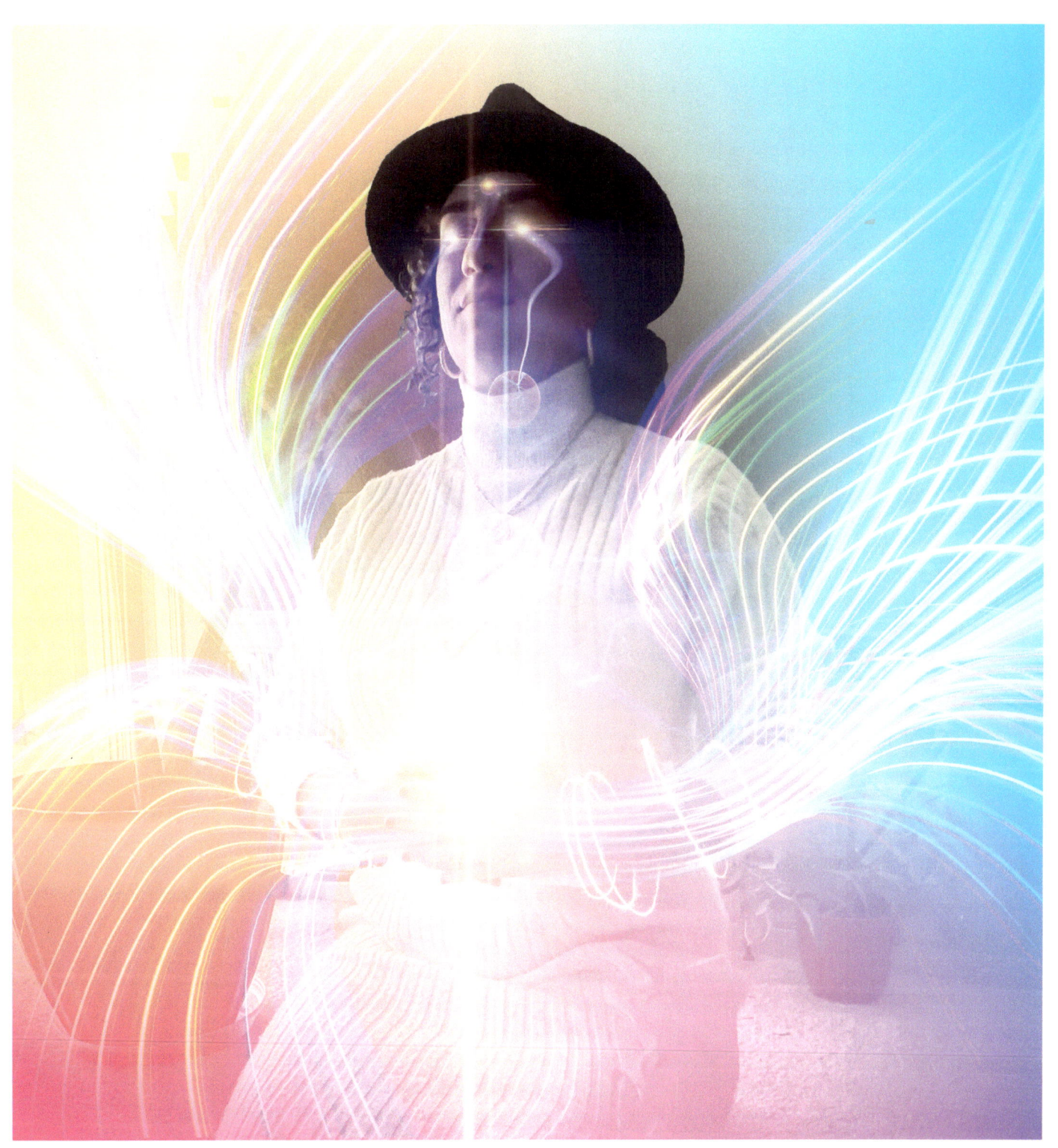

Reiki with Yvonne

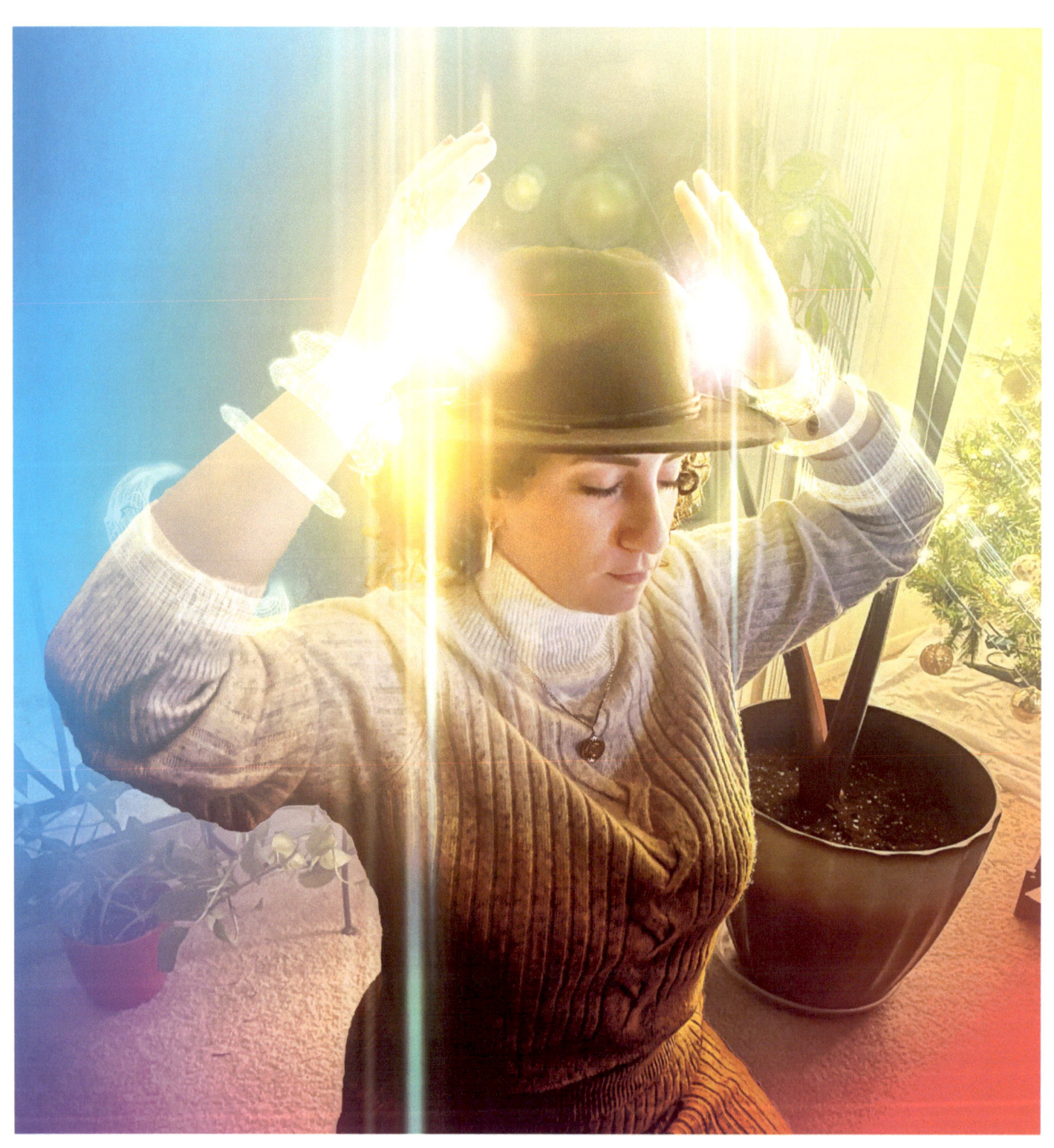

Reihi with Yvonne 3

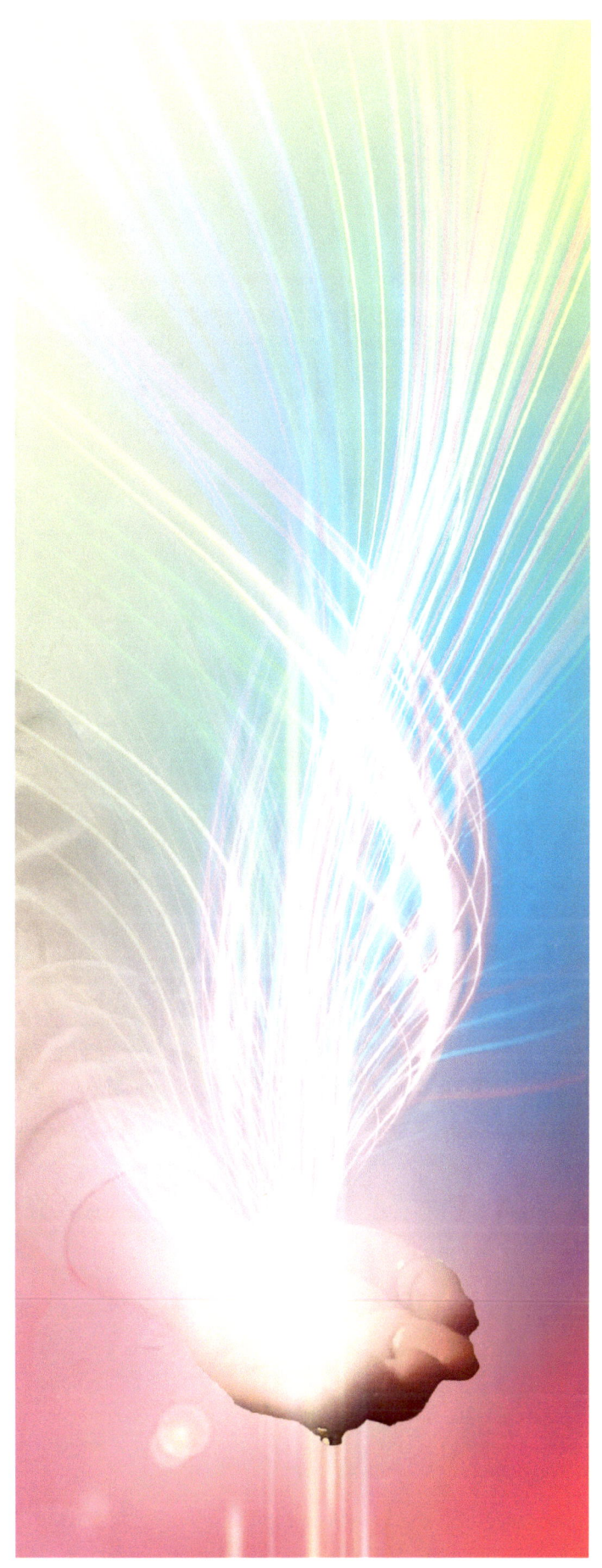

Reihi with Yvonne 4

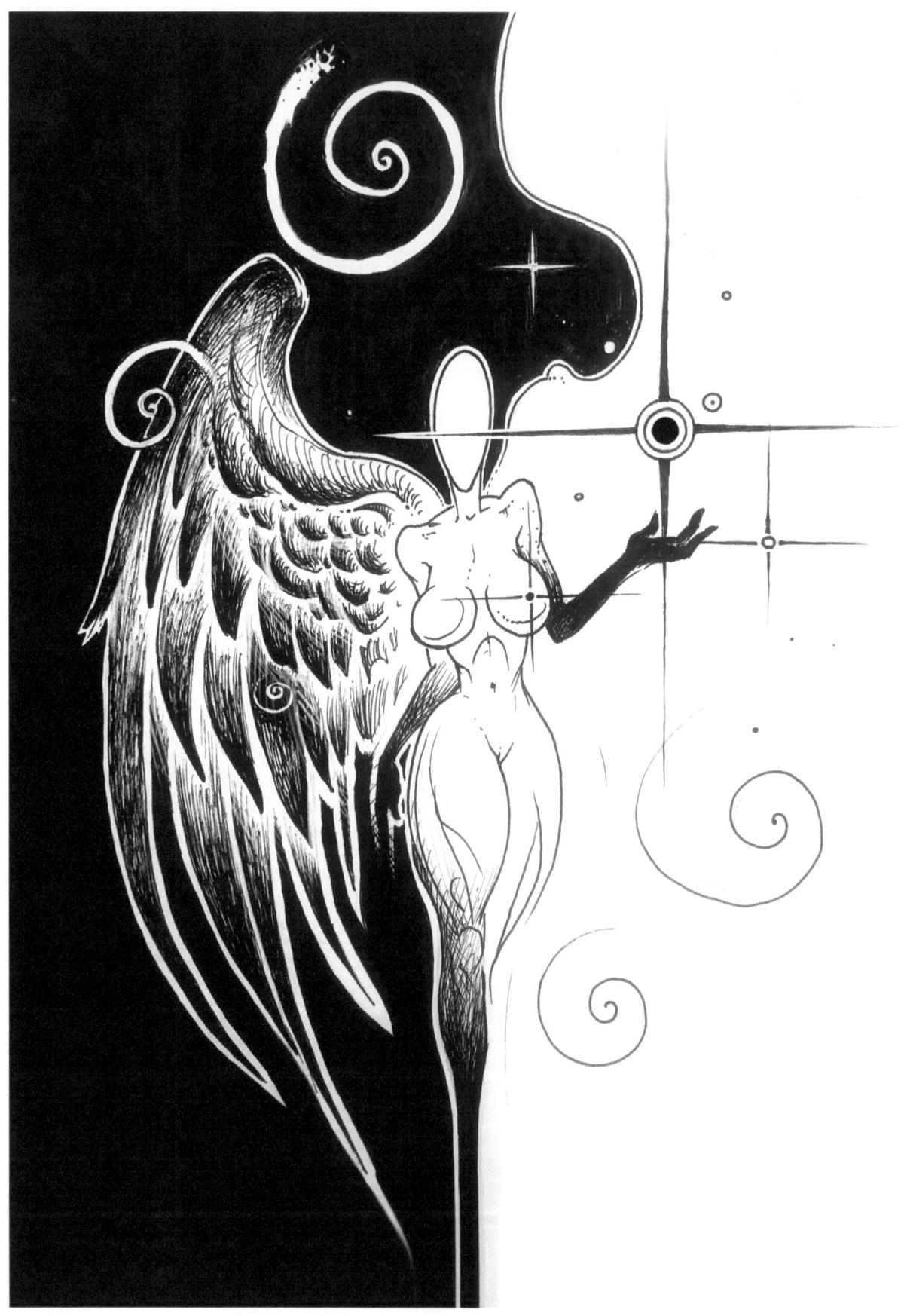

Kween

Due to her wing-like forms, she is the fastest of the four GALAXAVIORS. She is also the youngest.

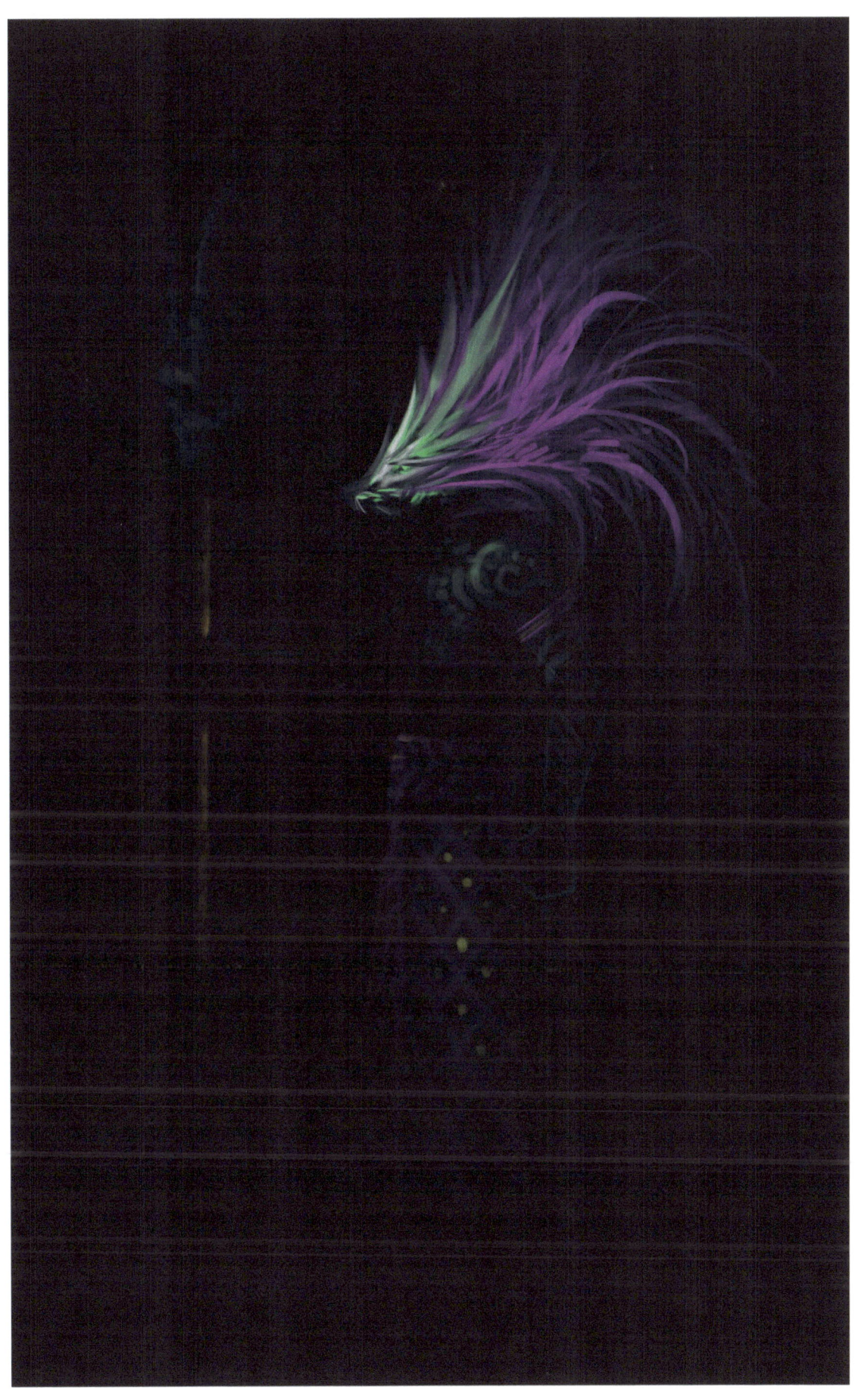

Tribal King

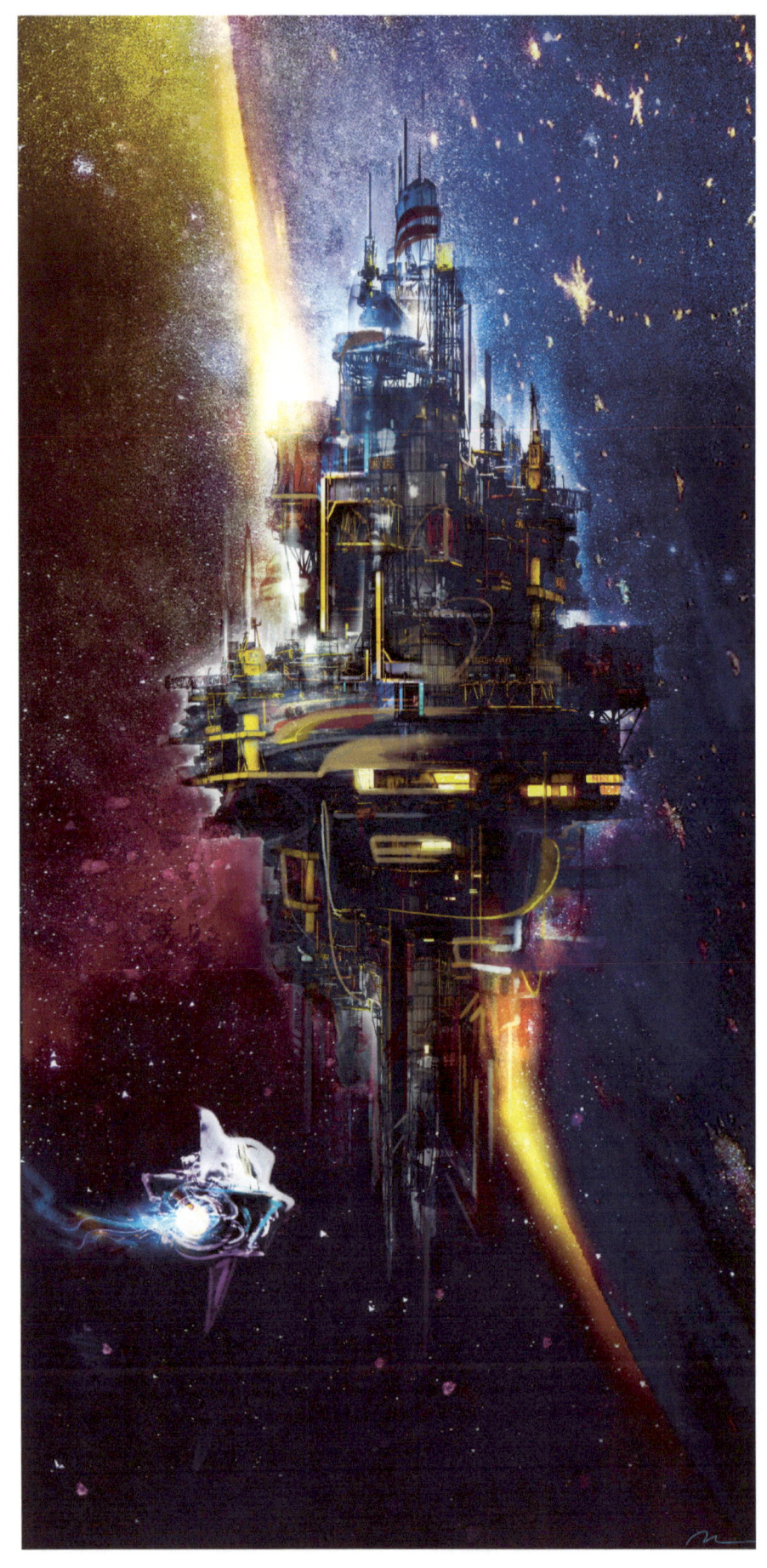

Ship City

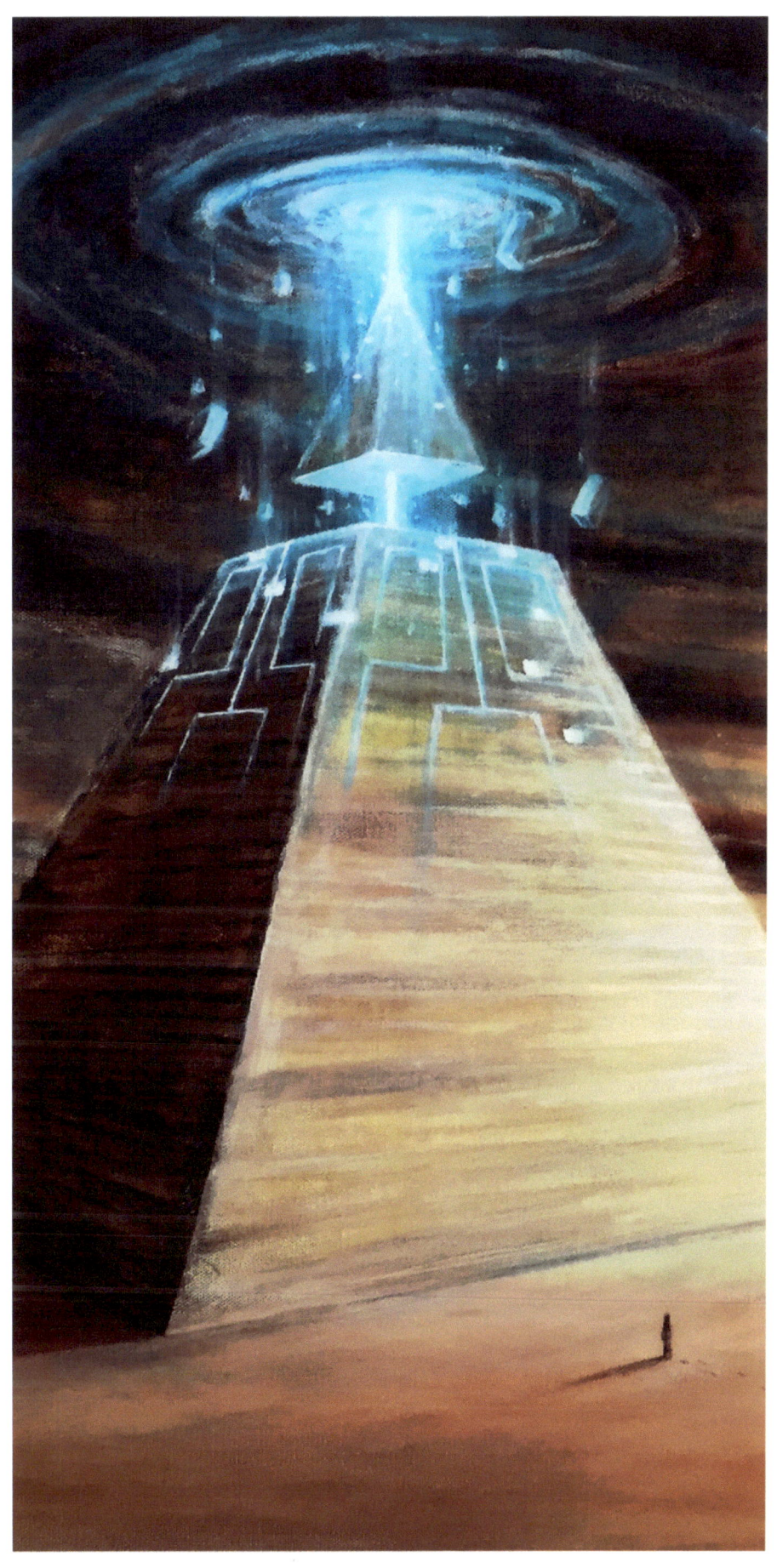

Aliens Built The Pyramids?

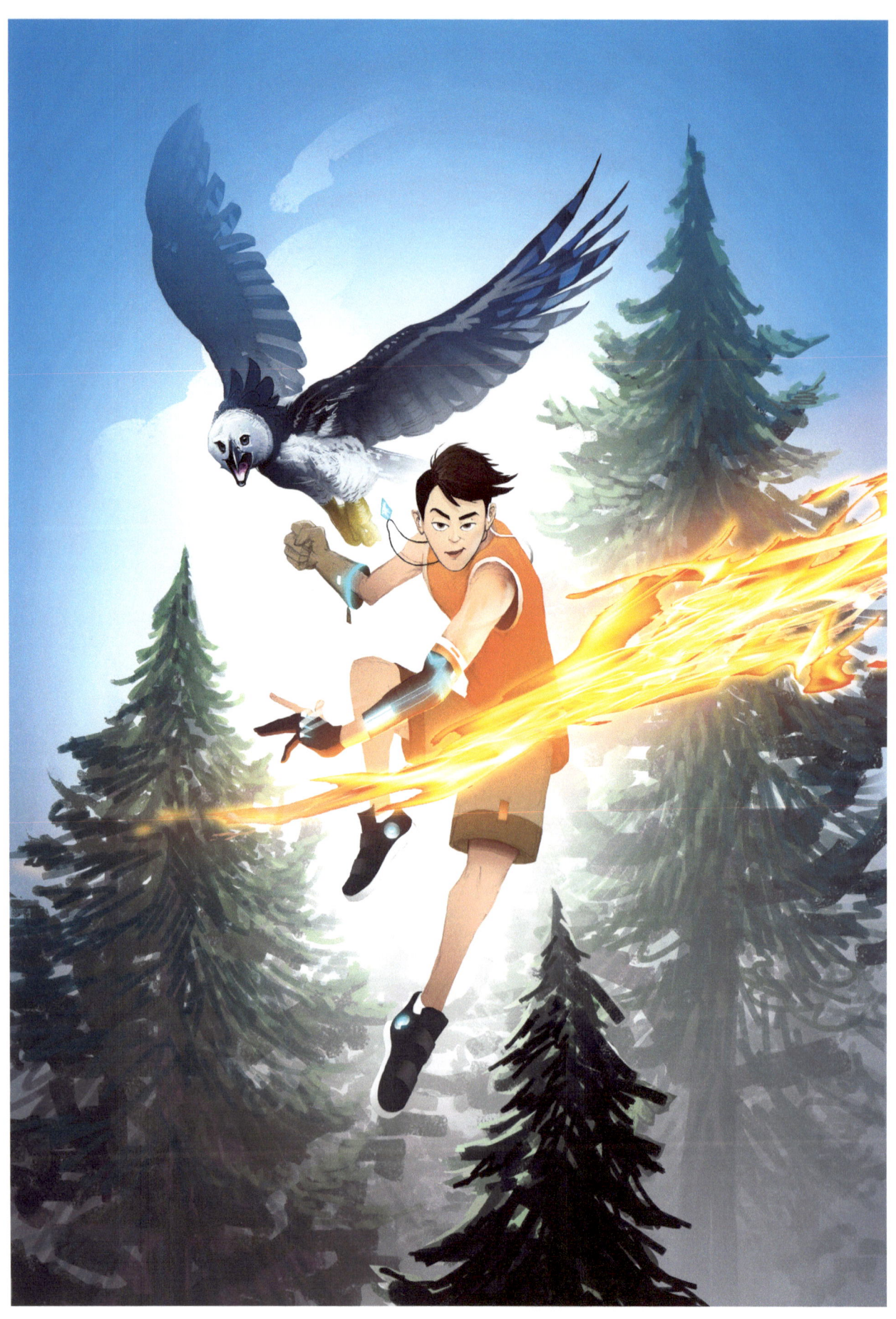

Hartly and Valley

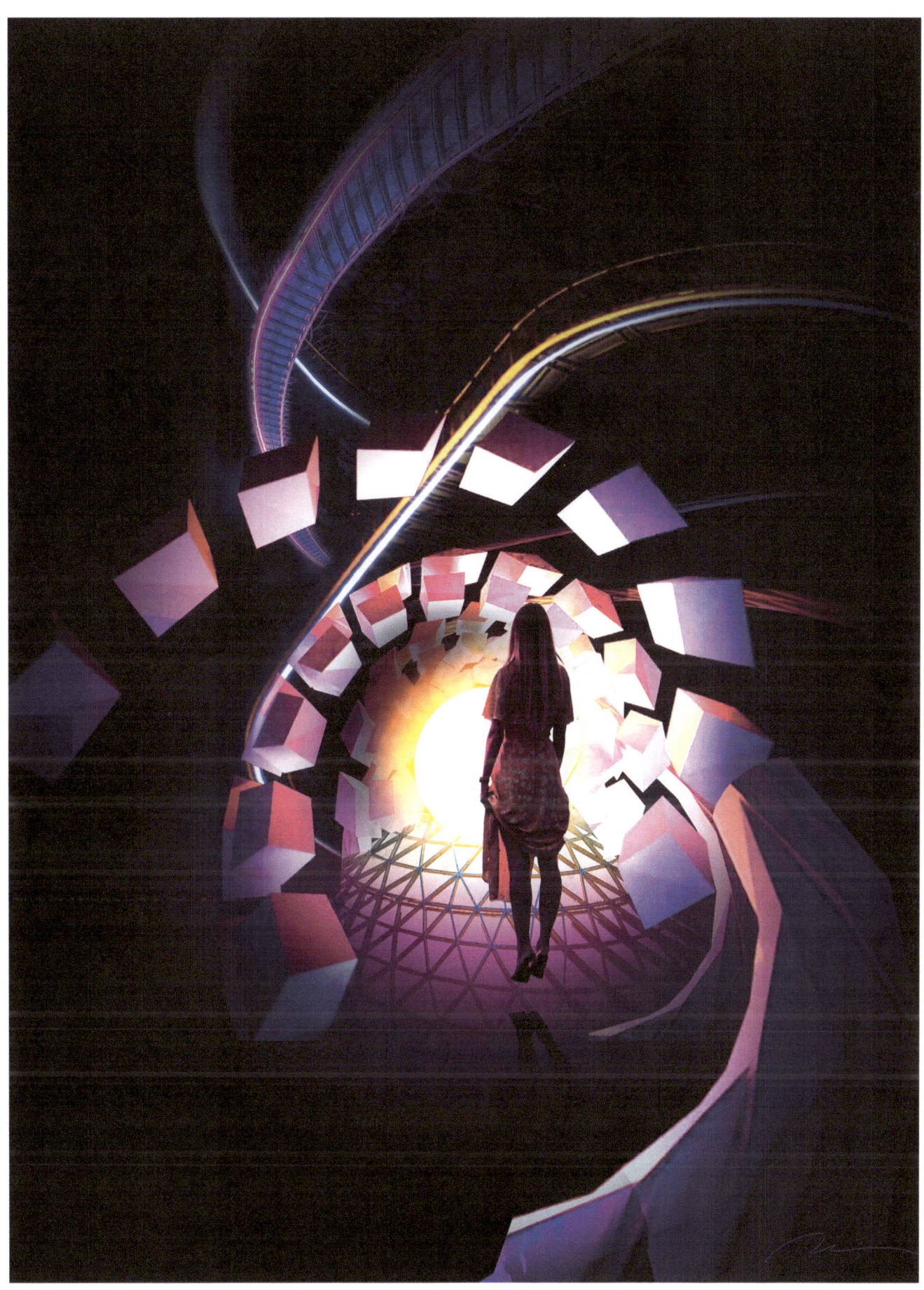

Eye Am

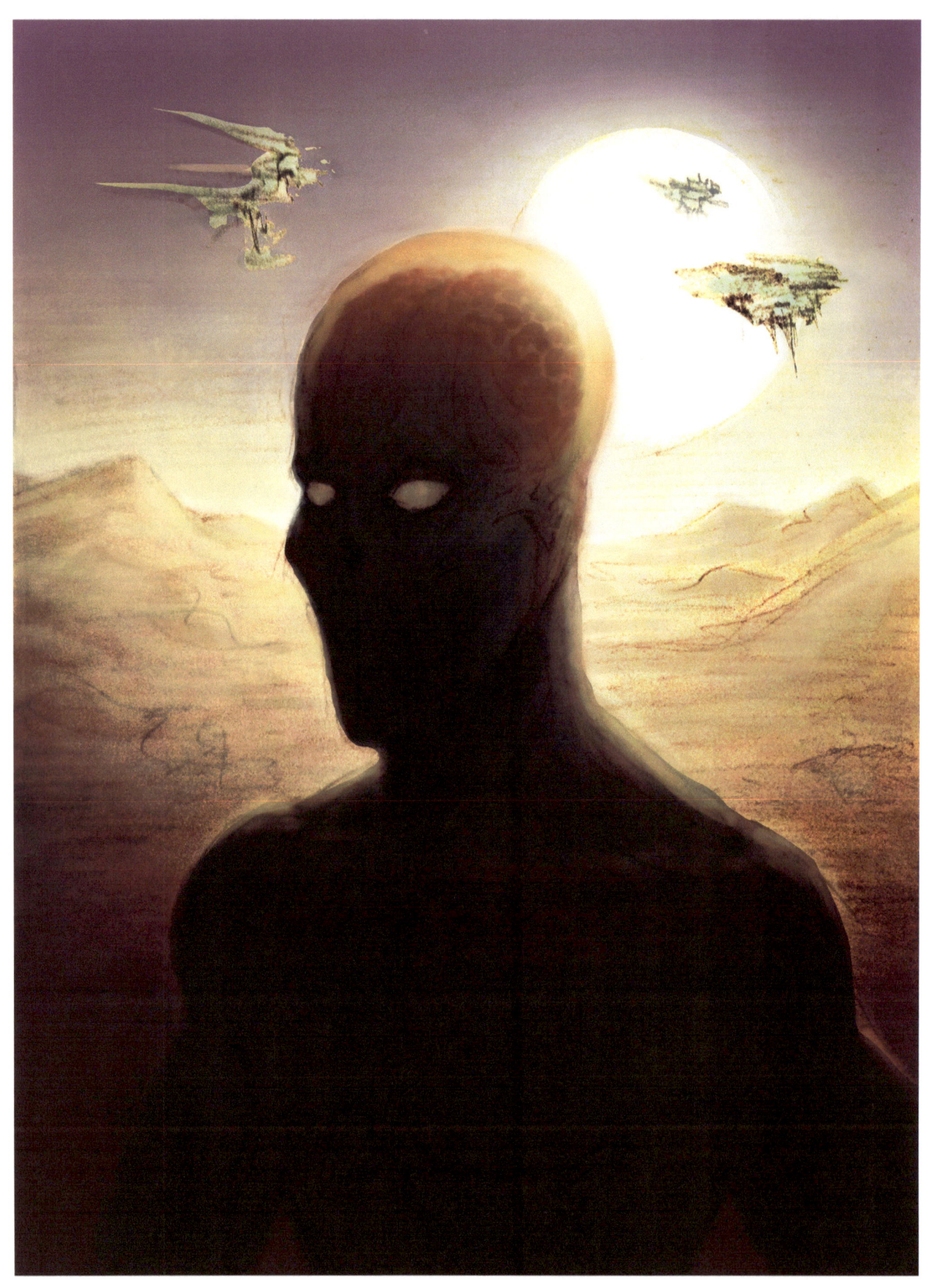

Subsurface Intelligence

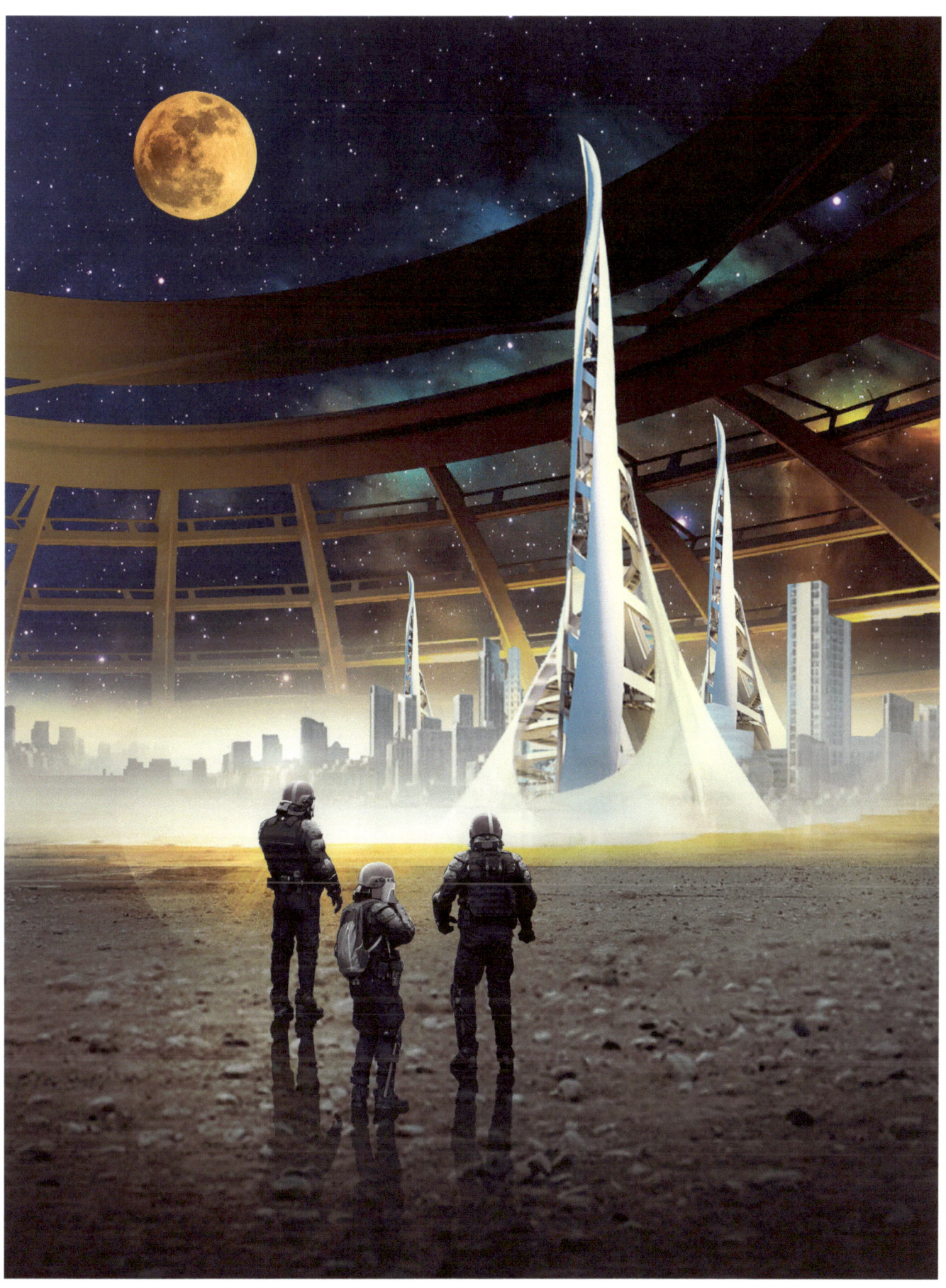

Punk World

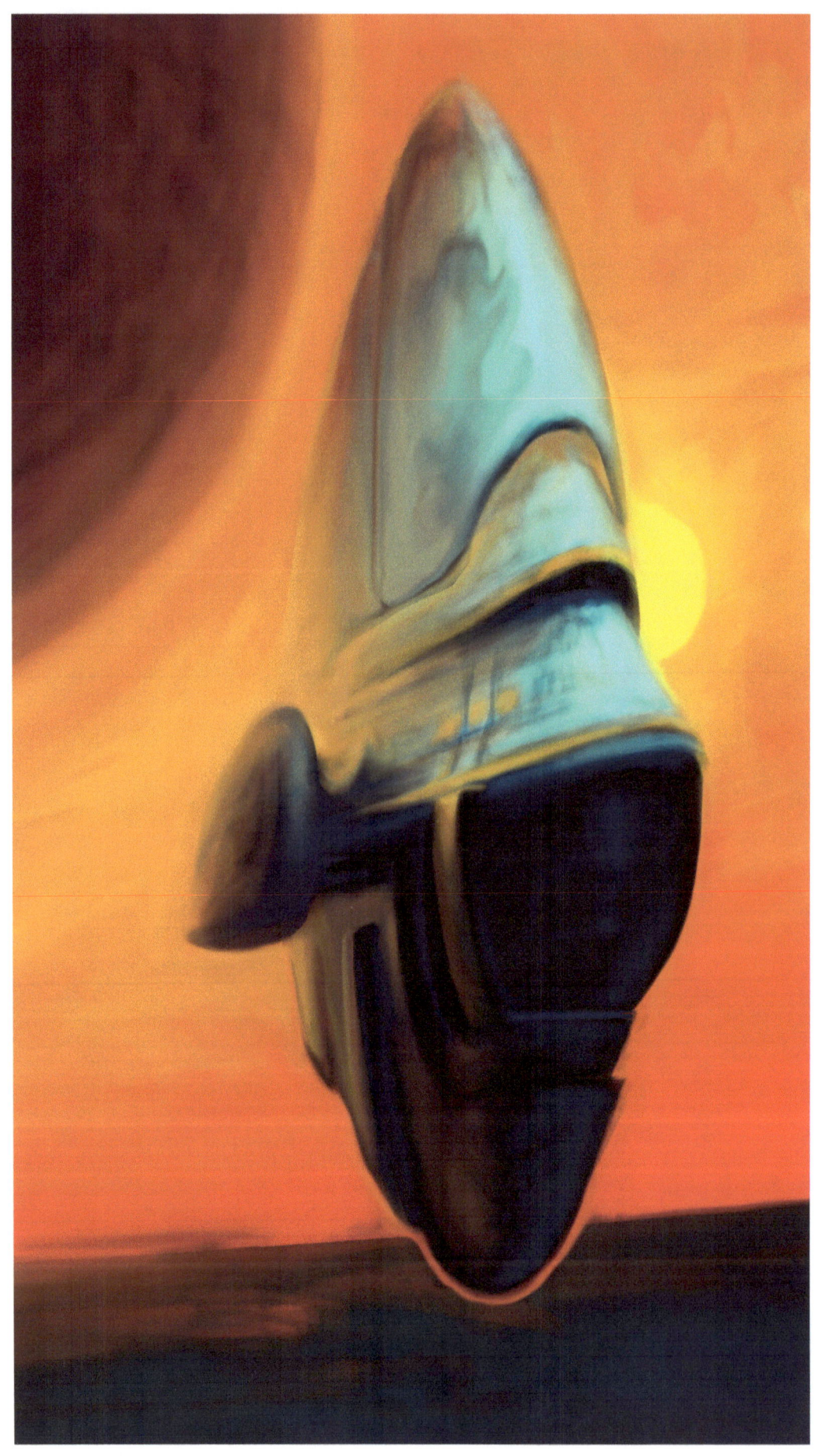

Fish Ship

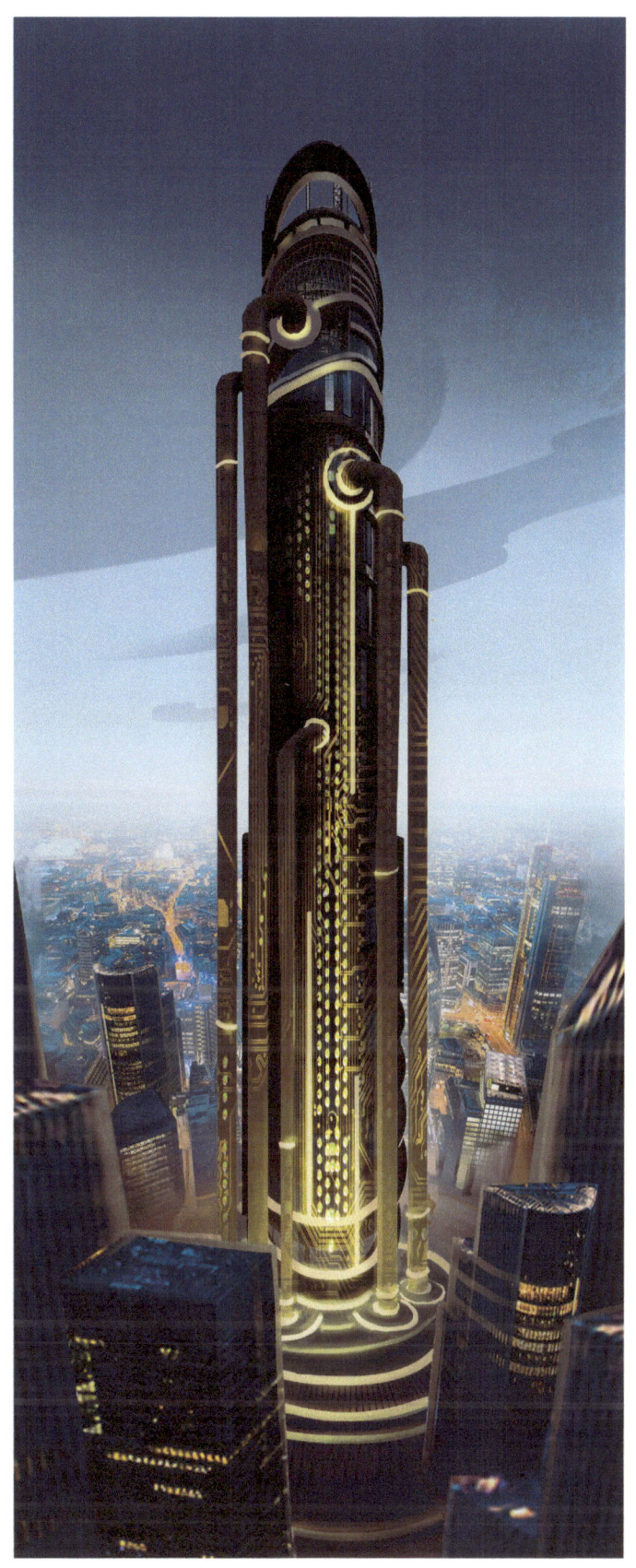

The Battery

A building that acts as the battery to the city.
Fueling everything with a new and unknown
power source... For free.

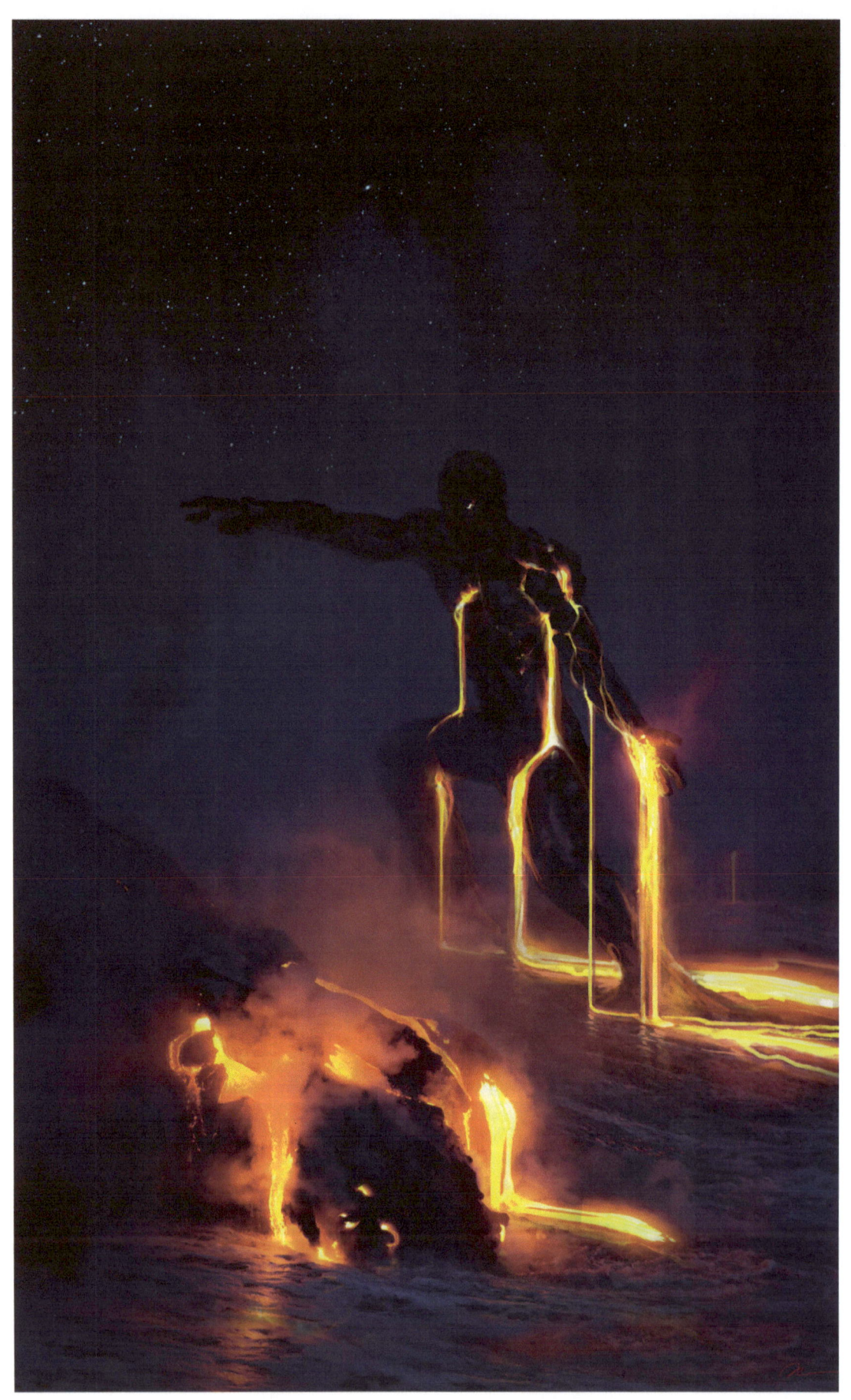

The Only Way Out Is Through

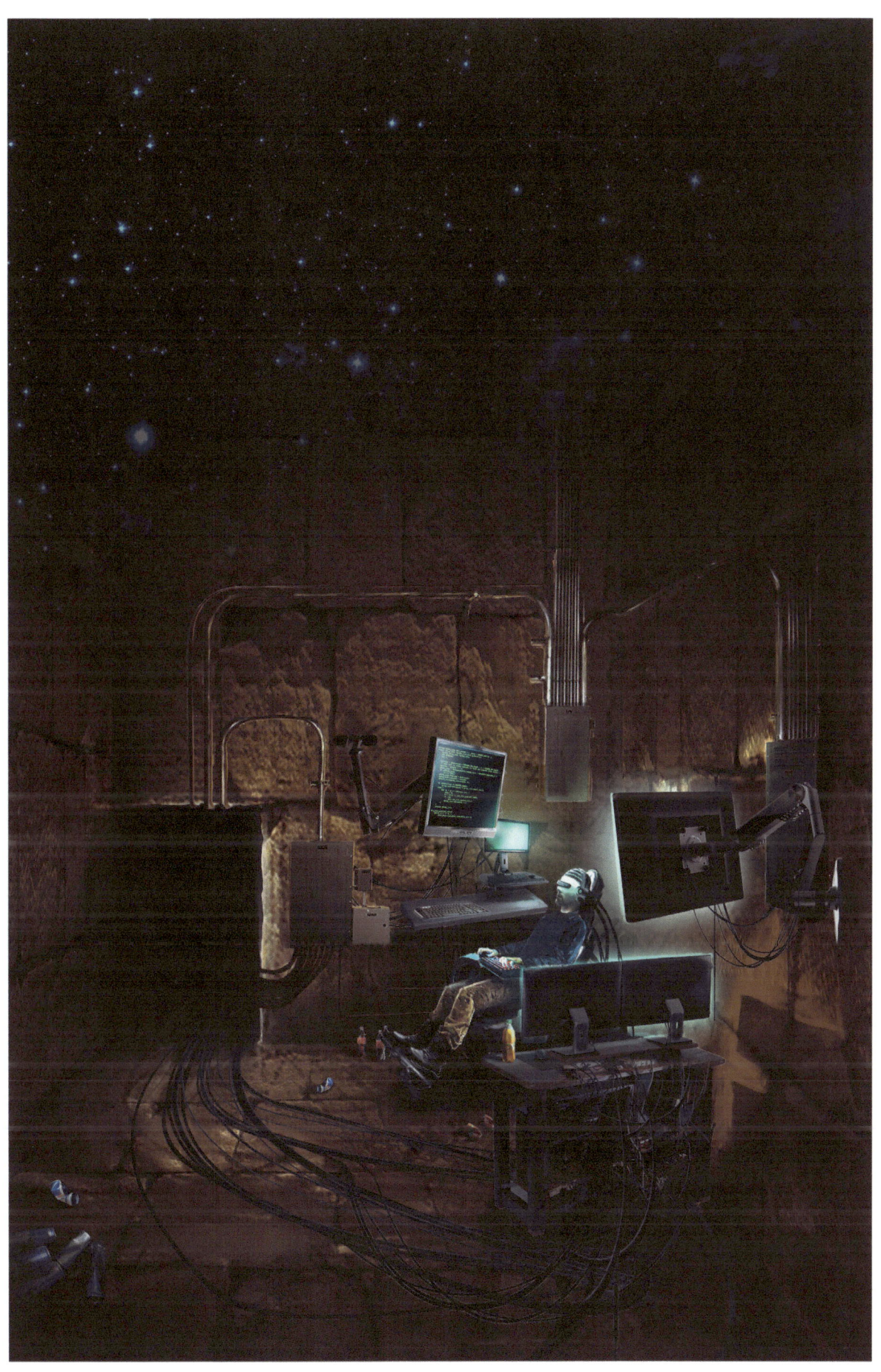

Dream Hacker

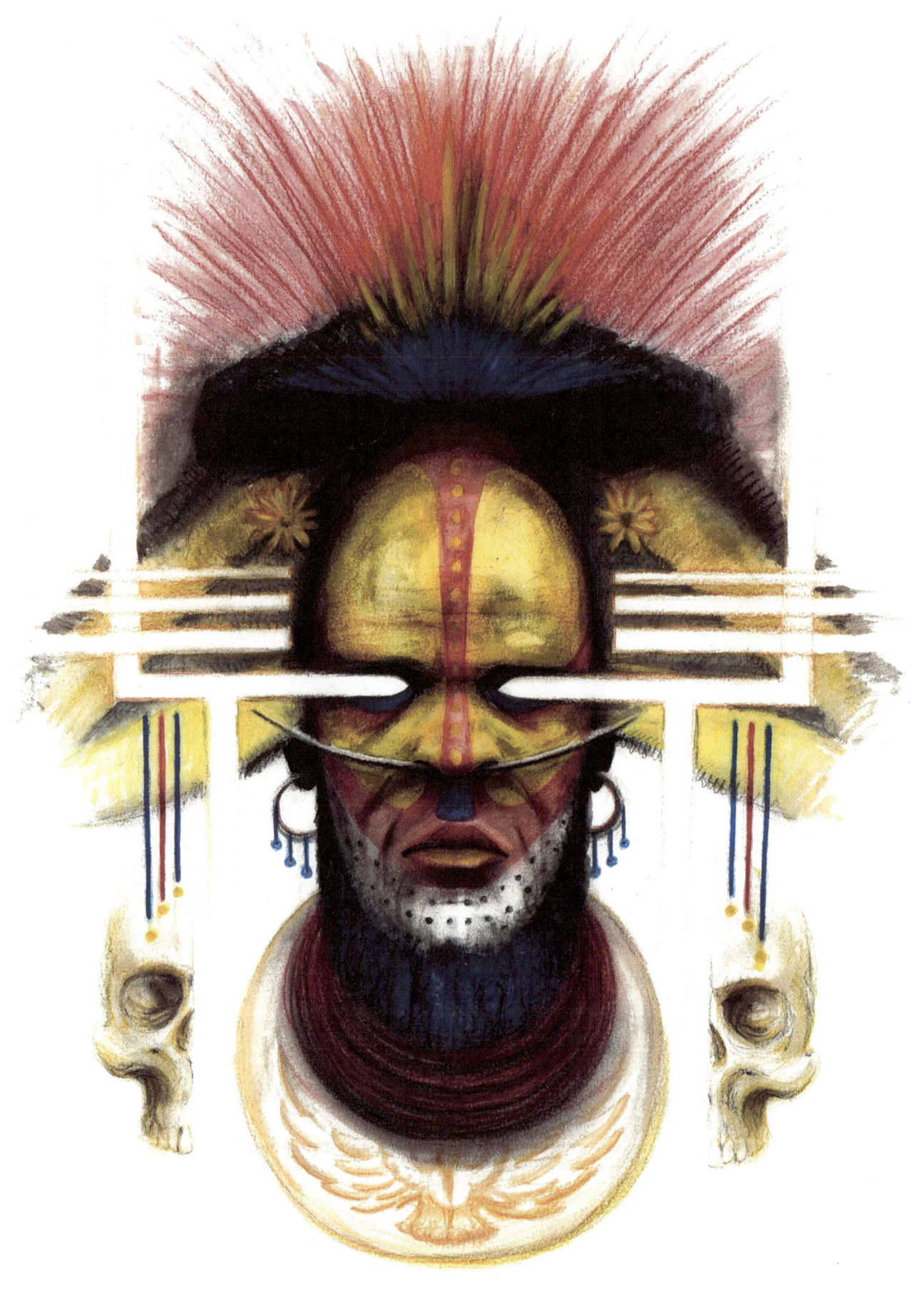

The Native